Praise

'I love this book; it's fast paced and really practical.
The exercises are incredibly insightful, and I know
it's going to be a must-read recommendation for all
my clients.'
— **Karen Skidmore**, business catalyst and
creator of the Grow Strong™ Principles

'Sharing my story, warts and all, has given me and
my family a life we never expected to have and a
business that has impacted hundreds of thousands of
people around the world. You have a story to share
too.

'The challenge is knowing how to weave your
experiences, values and thoughts into stories that
make a difference to your bottom line. In this book,
Susan solves that problem and shows you that, if
you apply the lessons within, you can build a loyal
following, effortlessly generate great clients and have
fun while doing it!

'In a world that can feel disconnected, this book will
help you connect with the right people, and maybe
even change your business and life in the process. I
wish you the best of luck.'
— **Dan Meredith**, entrepreneur and
international bestselling author of *How to be
F***ing Awesome*

'I'm delighted that Susan has blended her passion for storytelling with her immense talent for writing in this incredible book. "Storytelling" is the buzzword in marketing these days, but no one's telling you how to do it. Or, if they are, they're making it really complicated! This book is practical, and the exercises are insightful and powerful. Susan is a master storyteller and explains it like no one else.'

— **Richard Woods**, award-winning entrepreneur, BBC's *The Apprentice* personality and double bestselling author

'I've read a lot of books on storytelling for business and have always been left feeling overwhelmed and confused... until now. Susan's Circles of Storytelling Magic methodology is so clever and easy to get your head around; the pace and flow of her book is perfect and peppered with story examples and insightful exercises. Susan makes you realise that the stories you need to tell are all there; you just needed her guidance to discover them. Every business owner should read this book!'

— **Jill Pryor**, brand designer and mentor, Blossom Lane Creatives

'Finally, a book about storytelling that shows you how to do it! Susan has created a game-changing framework for entrepreneurs who want to grab attention, be memorable and connect with their customers through powerful stories.'

— **Monica Sood**, brand story coach, Monicaink

'At last, a practical guide that will enable thousands of business owners to tell their story with more confidence, greater resonance and enhanced clarity. Susan has a unique take on how to tell better stories and an easy-to-follow model, so if you have struggled in the past to clearly articulate your story, there is no excuse now. She has created a concise "how to" manual to make the whole brand articulation challenge both doable and logical. I will be encouraging my clients and network to buy this book and embrace Susan's model.'

— **Nick Cramp**, business transformation coach and author of *Better Before Bigger*

The Business of Stories

Harness the power of storytelling to demonstrate your value, attract your ideal clients and get paid what you're worth

SUSAN PAYTON

R^ethink

To my two gorgeous girls

Contents

Foreword

Who doesn't love a transformation story? In fact, transformation is at the heart of all classic stories. We go on an imaginative, emotional journey with the protagonist as they hear the call, set out on their quest, slay a few dragons and save the day. By 'The End' they have surprised and surpassed themselves, and transformed into heroine or hero.

In the world of coaching there is nothing more exhilarating than witnessing transformation in the people we work with. One of my favourite 'aha' moments in the transformation stakes is when a client really, *really gets* that their story is their greatest asset.

In *The Business of Stories*, author Susan Payton takes us to another transformational level altogether, awakening

1

us to our own story prowess. It's a great shake-up and wake-up call – personally and professionally. Susan invites us into a process of exploration and discovery about how our stories create the ground upon which we stand and serve as our own true north for personal meaning and purpose. More critically to her point, we discover that our stories are the means to our successful business development and income growth.

There are a lot of well-meaning voices out there, from coaches to marketing experts, telling us that we *should* tell stories and telling us *why* we should tell stories. We need more than that. Finally, along comes Susan Payton to show us *how!*

With years of passionate listening to client stories around the globe, and rigorous experimentation and research, Susan artfully takes us by the hand and shows us how to craft three key stories – the personal story, the business story and the customer story – and the alchemy of leveraging them to create connection, the gold dust for attracting one's ideal clients.

As part of my responsibility as foreword writer, I must alert readers to a marvellous contradiction about this book. On the one hand, Susan invites us to take our time, not to rush, to invest and immerse ourselves slowly and thoughtfully. She seductively beckons us into a 'retreat-in-a-book' that is spiritual, philosophical and motivational. On the other hand, she writes with such affirming energy and practicality, you feel the cattle prod of the coach calling you to action. I couldn't get through a page without my highlighter pen and voicing aloud, 'Yes! That's *it*!' I couldn't wait to dive into each exercise and come up for air with handfuls of pearls to be cultivated.

Anyone remember the iconic fantasy film, *Field of Dreams*? The hero, a farmer in the American Midwest, played by Kevin Costner, follows the call of an inner voice saying, 'Build it and they will come.' He builds a baseball diamond in the middle of his cornfield. Magically, all the baseball legends of his youth come to play on it.

I can't think of a more apt analogy for Susan Payton's central premise: craft the right story and your ideal clients will come.

Dr Diana Theodores
Director, Theatre 4 Business
Author, *Performing as You: How to have authentic impact in every role you play*
🔗 www.linkedin.com/in/d1ana

Introduction

What if...

What if you had a story that someone else could learn from and be inspired by?

What if your story, with its ups and downs, bumps and bruises, successes and failures, touched someone deeply and inspired them to keep going?

What if the low points of your story gave someone else hope, or optimism, or the courage to step up and follow their dream?

What if the bits of your story that make you feel vulnerable gave someone else strength?

What if your openness and honesty created a space where someone else felt they too could be open and honest?

Wouldn't it be a tragedy if that story was never told?

We all have stories to tell

Marion Ellis wanted to tell her story, but she wasn't sure how to.

'I love stories,' she told me. 'Who doesn't? I know telling my story could really help me connect with my ideal client but,' she sighed, 'I don't know which stories to tell, or how much I should share, or even how to tell them so that my clients want to engage with them.'

There are a lot of Marions. I've had the same conversation with many business owners over the last few years, from founders and freelancers to coaches and consultants, all experts in their field who understand the importance of storytelling but feel utterly confused about where to start, let alone how to 'master the art'.

It's a minefield.

Maybe you've tried but were disappointed that no one engaged. Maybe you've given it a good go but got little or no response. Maybe it felt awkward or forced.

I feel your pain. No one wants to do it badly or tell stories for the sake of it. That would be 'dumping' – or therapy! I get it. I founded The Business of Stories back in 2016 because I get it.

The problem is, if you're not doing it, your marketing could be completely out of kilter with the people and work you want more of. You could be attracting the 'wrong' clients, getting work you don't love or finding sales conversations excruciatingly uncomfortable.

That's exactly where I was a few years ago.

I had launched a group called The Business of Mums, offering coaching to help members get their new businesses up and running, but it was hard. I was struggling to get clients because I wasn't giving people anything to connect with. I was busy delivering a ton of useful content that lots of people were engaging with, but I found it difficult to get anyone to actually buy, and I ended up doing work that didn't light me up.

In desperation, I spent a ridiculous amount of money with a local marketing agency, but it didn't help. Nothing was working. Until, that is, I told my story.

It might sound dramatic, but telling my story completely transformed my business, and my life. From the moment I started sharing it, people – some of whom had been members of my online community for months but had never engaged with it – were responding and posting in my group. Many commented on how much they related to my story and thanked me for inspiring them to embrace and share theirs. I was no longer just a name. They got what I was about. They felt a connection.

Why does that matter? Because when people feel connected to you, they'll trust you to help them. Several people messaged me to ask about working with me, and within days I had more paying clients than I had had in the previous six months. I was blown away.

Sharing my story was such a game-changing experience for me that I got busy telling everyone who would listen to 'harness the power of storytelling'. I soon realised, though, that while lots of business owners bought into the idea and wanted to do it, they struggled to know how.

I get that too. If writing isn't your 'thing', you may not feel confident that you could craft a story that will attract your ideal clients, build meaningful connections, create raving fans and elevate your brand. That's fine. Don't worry. I'm going to show you that storytelling doesn't need to be hard – or scary – and take you step-by-step through a process to reveal the three key stories you need to unpack first:

1. **Your personal story** – who you are, how you got to where you are now and why it matters

2. **Your business story** – what your business stands for and what problem it exists to solve

3. **Your customer story** – who they are and where *you* fit into *their* story

Unpacking those stories will give you a ton of clarity and a deeper understanding of your own motivations, your business proposition and your target market.

Then, you'll discover that between your personal story and your business story lies your *why*: the reason you do what you do. Between your business story and your customer story lies your *value*: how you help your customers win. And, between your personal story and your customer story you'll find your *people*: the 'ideal' clients you feel passionately called to serve.

And that's not all. As these stories start to merge and overlap, you'll find the sweet spot in the middle where there is pure goosebump-inducing *magic* just waiting to happen. It's why I call my process The Circles of Storytelling Magic.

From that sweet spot, you can write words that will sing to the person you want to work with; music that will fill their heart so that working with *you* feels like a perfect fit. When your ideal clients hear your stories, they'll be captivated. Spellbound. They'll stop shopping around, because they'll know they've found 'the one'.

Don't worry if you've never considered yourself a storyteller. You don't need to be an expert copywriter or super-talented wordsmith. I'm going to show you how you can quickly and easily become proficient in the universal language of storytelling, so you can stop worrying that you're doing it wrong and, instead, feel confident that you know how to inject a little storytelling magic into all your marketing.

Together, we'll unearth your unique treasure chest of precious stories and compile the ones you're going to share. We'll look at writing tips, structure, how to start and end your stories, and how to inject them with personality. I'll be sharing resources, tips and templates I've put together over many years as a storyteller, copywriter, messaging geek and, since the beginning of 2019, a StoryBrand Certified Guide.

I'll walk you through the process and some of the exercises I've been taking clients through since 2016 and, with their permission, share some of their stories – so you'll have lots of real-life examples to bring the process and exercises to life.

Clients like Marion.

Exciting plans and a big vision

Marion was an expert in her field. She had qualified as a chartered surveyor in 2004 and had twenty+ years' experience in the residential property sector.

She'd worked in both corporate and small to medium-sized enterprise environments, before getting off the exhausting treadmill and working for herself.

Marion truly understood the challenges faced by many in her profession and was feeling called to create a community to provide support, coaching and connection for those in her industry who didn't want to have to figure everything out on their own.

She had exciting plans and a big vision; she wanted to make an impact; she wanted to start a movement; but she wasn't sure how to go out to her audience and talk about it, what her core message should be or what stories she should tell.

Working with the process I'm going to take you through in this book, Marion got the clarity she needed. She deepened her understanding of the value she provided and how to share her personal story in a way that felt totally aligned with her brand and the kind of purpose-driven individuals she wanted to work with.

With her newfound clarity, and feedback from her ideal clients that they totally resonated with her message, she confidently launched a community, a website, her first mastermind and an engaging brand that was a perfect fit for her and her audience.

Everything felt congruent and true to who she was and what she wanted her business to stand for. Her business was able to grow and thrive, because getting clear on her stories had ensured she connected with the right audience to make it happen.

That's what I want for you.

This book is designed to demystify the sometimes overly complicated 'art' of storytelling and equip you with a simple, practical way to craft and share stories like a pro. Work through it in order and you will have everything you need to tell the stories that will attract your ideal clients in a way that feels aligned and true to who you are and what you stand for. I'll also show you all sorts of other magical things that can happen when you share the right stories in the right way, such as attracting more of the people you love working with, no longer having to compete on price (or compete at all) and actually enjoying sales conversations, without ever feeling 'salesy'.

Be sure to enjoy the process. Take it step by step, and you'll sharpen your storytelling skills as you go. Storytelling is fun. It's magical. It's a superpower.

I would recommend you don't jump ahead. You may want to read through the book to get a feel for the journey and where it's all leading you, but then work through it, chapter by chapter, as it follows a logical order. Some steps may be quick for you, some you may need to spend longer on, so give yourself the space to do that. I highly recommend you block some time off in your schedule so that you can think, reflect and get lost in the joy of storytelling – without all the distractions of a busy modern life.

 You'll find a companion workbook waiting for you at www.thebusinessofstories.com/magic. Print it off now so that, as you work through this book, you can capture your thoughts and ideas, ready for when we craft and share your stories in Part Three.

Now that you can see what the journey we're going on together looks like you can relax, trust the process, enjoy the ride and know that you've got this. If you're ready to stop wasting your precious time, money and energy on marketing that isn't working for you, and instead attract your ideal clients with the simple magic of storytelling, I'm ready to show you how.

Let's do this!

PART ONE: UNPACK

Getting your stories out of your head and into the open

1
The Simple Magic Of Storytelling

Heathrow, Terminal 5

In February 2019, I was sitting in Heathrow Airport, drinking a latte and feeling a little tearful. I had chosen an adventure that led to me getting ready to board a plane to Nashville, Tennessee, USA. Flying over 4,000 miles away on my own, I would be leaving my husband, two daughters and two dogs behind for a week.

As I sat watching the world go by, I posted on LinkedIn. No image. No video. Just a short post that started, 'Sitting in Heathrow Terminal 5, feeling a little tearful. It's a mix of emotions...'

By the time I got back a week later, that post had had over 17,000 views, ninety-four comments and several private messages. My invitations to connect on

LinkedIn had shot up, visits to my website had spiked and a flurry of people had downloaded my free guide (even though I hadn't mentioned it in my post). Several people had booked a call via my online scheduler to talk about working with me on my return.

What was the post that instigated all of that activity? I had shared how brave my little girl had been when I dropped her at school that morning, knowing she wouldn't see me for a week, and how I was feeling quite tearful from the mix of emotions – both nervous and super excited, all at the same time. It was short, but real and honest. I hadn't written it to win business, but I got clients from that one post.

Never underestimate the power of a story.

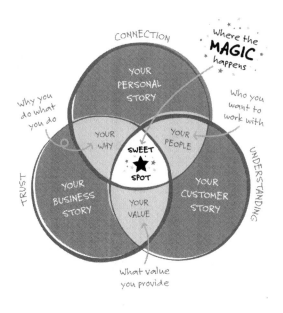

All the stories

When I talk about storytelling, I'm not just referring to the 'one story'. You know, the one you've put on your 'About' page or tell at the beginning of every talk you do. I'm talking about *all* the stories.

Everything about your business is potentially a story: the way you do what you do; the project you're working on right now; the clients you're working with and the results they've had. All stories. You might not tell them all; some you might tell often, some you might only tell to certain audiences or in certain situations, and some you might tell once, but you have a million stories to choose from and you're creating new ones every day. Please put aside the idea that you don't have stories, or that you're no good at telling them, or that no one is interested in them. That is simply not true.

Your stories are living breathing things. They're not static pieces of copy; they come in all shapes and sizes and can be conveyed in many ways. You get to choose which ones you want to share; the purpose of this book is to help you be more intentional, mindful and skilful at unpacking your stories, exploring the gold that lives within them, and deciding how and where you're going to share them so that they connect with your ideal client.

My own storytelling journey has been an exciting adventure. Everything I'm doing today – the business I now have, the clients I get to work with, the ambitious goals I've achieved, including writing these words and publishing this book – started with me taking a deep breath and telling my own story. A story that has had the inevitable ups and downs, successes and failures, happy times and hard times. But that's life, isn't it? We all experience highs and lows.

Back in 2015, when I first started sharing my story, my 'highs' included a beautiful daughter, who gave me a compelling reason to get up every morning and make every day count, and an exciting job in media. I worked in the press office at TV-am (anyone remember Anne and Nick?) and later at Capital Radio, a station that was 'Number one in London by miles and miles' – or so the jingle went. I also worked with Chris Tarrant for many years, organised fundraising balls, dinners and other events in and around London, and attended premieres, opening nights and exclusive events, often with VIP and backstage passes.

But the 'lows' were an important part of my story too, including the guilt I felt at leaving my daughter with someone else while I commuted into central London to work. I gave my childminder a little book to write notes in each day, so I would know what they'd done, the funny things my daughter had said, what she'd eaten. But looking through that little book each night made me sad. I was reading about her life instead of being there, living it with her.

I became a single mum on my daughter's sixth birthday and then, for many years, suffered from chronic fatigue. One of my lowest moments was standing at the bottom of a flight of stairs in a cinema in Epsom, Surrey, crying because I didn't have the energy to walk up them to watch a film with my then ten-year-old.

Another was steadily building up a property portfolio to ensure I could provide the life I wanted for my daughter, only to find myself hundreds of thousands of pounds in debt when the property market crashed in 2007.

Being heard

There's a really important point I want to make before we move on. The impact telling my story has had on my business was not down to its content. I didn't have some humdinger of a tale that was fit for a Hollywood blockbuster. Far from it. It was just a story that, in some part, many of the 1,500-plus business owners I told it to back in 2015 related to.

Some were also single parents working hard to provide for their family. Some were business owners who'd burnt the midnight oil and, as a result, burnt out – like I had. Some were would-be entrepreneurs who'd invested in a business venture, only to find themselves heavily in debt or bankrupt.

Many simply related to the fact that we all accumulate bumps and bruises along the way. At times, life feels good and in flow, and at other times, it's bloody tough and stormy. Just as these people related to something in my story, others will relate to something in yours.

The difference my story made was down to what happened when I told it. I went from struggling to cut through the noise to being heard. I went from not knowing how to attract the people I wanted to work with to having ideal clients reach out to me. I went from being just another moderator of a group to being a real human with a story that connected with other humans, because something in it was meaningful to them.

One comment

It was 7pm on Thursday 26 May 2016 when I heard the comment that would completely change the trajectory of my business. I was at a monthly peer-to-peer mentoring session at my local university, and someone was saying they had been invited to do a talk – and they weren't sure what to talk about.

As usual, I was recounting what had happened to me when I told my story and commented that their own story would be a great subject for their talk. The business start-up manager, who was facilitating the session, agreed.

'Storytelling is so important,' he said. 'I've been thinking I'd like to add a new module to our business start-up course on that very topic.'

'Oh wow, that's brilliant,' I enthused. 'I'd love to hear that. Any chance I could come and sit at the back of the room for that one?'

He looked at me. 'Hmmm, well,' he said, 'I was kinda hoping you'd be at the front of the room – delivering it.' He laughed and carried on talking, but I never heard another word. To say a lightbulb had gone on in my head was an understatement. This was one of those jaw-dropping, stop-me-in-my-tracks, 'oh-my-God-did-he-just-say-what-I-think-he-said, could-this-actually-be-a-thing?' 'aha' moments.

I drove home from that meeting with a smile from ear to ear. How had I not seen this before? It was so obvious. This was it. I had finally found my thing. My love of storytelling had started at a young age but, in that moment, it dawned on me that I could turn that love into a living.

From then on, everything fell into place ridiculously quickly. In the following *eight days*, a series of events played out so brilliantly, I managed to create a website, a brochure, a process and a talk, which I (nervously) delivered to forty entrepreneurs in London just over one week later.

From that first talk, I got six paying clients and The Business of Stories was born.

The perfect mix

As I write this book, several years later, the journey that unfolded from that day has brought me back full circle. For the first couple of years, my storytelling work focused on helping business owners tell their story; how their life experiences have shaped who they are today; the journey they've been on and the defining moments along the way.

Then in 2018, I came across a book called *Building a StoryBrand* by Donald Miller.[1] In it, he outlines a marketing framework that helps businesses focus their messaging on their customer story. I loved the

---

1   D Miller, *Building a StoryBrand: Clarify your message so customers will listen* (HarperCollins Leadership, 2017)

framework and immediately implemented it into the work I was already doing with my clients. In February 2019, I took a step further when I flew out to the USA and trained to be a StoryBrand Certified Guide.

As I worked with clients over the next few years, helping them to implement the StoryBrand framework into their business, I saw that there was another layer of storytelling that I could bring from my earlier work to help business owners see how and where their own story fits into their customer's story. Your customer story is super important and definitely one to tell, but there is a special place for your story too – as long as it's told in the right way, at the right time, to the right people. In fact, having the perfect mix of personal, business and customer story is an extremely powerful way to create a meaningful connection with your audience.

But let's not jump ahead of ourselves. First things first.

The storyteller's hat

Set yourself up for success by coming to this process with a sense of wonder and adventure. I love the idea Todd Herman talks about in *The Alter Ego Effect* of putting on the 'hat' and persona of the person you need to be to get a task done.[2]

---

2   T Herman, *The Alter Ego Effect: The power of secret identities to transform your life* (HarperBus, 2019)

Think about the qualities you need to tap into to become a great storyteller:

- **Curiosity.** Bring a sense of wonder with you. Be intrigued about what might come up. Don't dismiss anything too quickly, be judgemental or expect stories to arrive perfectly tied up in a bow, ready to be shared. Just be open to exploring them for gold.

- **Intuition.** Tune into which stories you feel compelled to share. Notice which ones speak to you and pop into your head or even your dreams. Follow your gut and intuition. Notice the stories that make you feel something. If they make *you* feel something, there's a good chance they'll make your audience feel something too.

- **Creativity.** Engage your creative brain. Even if you don't consider yourself a creative person, when it comes to storytelling, you are. You already tell stories all day long; I'm simply going to show you how to uncover the stories in your unique Circles of Storytelling Magic and get intentional about the ones you share in your marketing.

- **Enthusiasm.** Enjoy the journey. Bring your most positive energy. Going through this process shouldn't feel like a chore or a tick-box exercise; it's an adventure. This process is about reflecting on your journey and seeing how your stories align and connect with the people you want to engage with and do business with.

You already have all of these qualities in abundance. If you're up for bringing them to this work, I'll provide the 'how-to' steps and together we'll craft stories that will attract your ideal clients so that they show up, ready to buy from you.

 Even the hardest of stories can be told in a way that inspires others.

I'm excited that you're here. We're about to embark on a wonderful journey together.

 ## Storytelling magic

- You have a ton of stories and you are creating new ones every day. Everything you do is a story. I'm going to help you choose the right ones to share.

- Storytelling can help you cut through the noise and be heard above the crowd in a way that feels aligned and true to who you are and what you stand for.

- Approach this process with a sense of wonder and adventure. Be curious. If it helps, imagine putting on the 'hat' of a storyteller to help you fully engage and enjoy it.

- The perfect mix of personal, business and customer story is an extremely powerful way to create a meaningful connection with your audience.

- Storytelling is not just essential in business; it's a superpower.

2

Your Personal Story

The elephant

The elephant caught her eye. It looked so majestic. It was a stunning piece. She walked over to take a better look. It was even more beguiling up close. She loved it.

Skye Holland saw the woman looking at her painting intently and wandered over to her. They started chatting. The woman was clearly taken by the exquisite work of art and Skye enjoyed telling her about it. The woman took one last long look at the elephant and then politely thanked Skye, telling her she would think about it.

The day came to a close and the woman hadn't returned.

*The next morning, Skye was back at the Afford-
able Art Fair in Battersea, South London. It was a
three-day event and this was day two. The doors had
barely opened when the woman appeared in front of
the painting again. This time, she was beaming. Skye
walked over to her, and the woman immediately told
her she'd looked on her website after returning home
last night. She'd admired some of her other work
before clicking on her 'About' page and reading her
story, totally resonating with it. Like Skye, she had
spent time living in South Africa and felt a deep connection to the wild animals in their natural habitats.*

*'I want the elephant!' she announced, clearly excited
to be taking the artwork home, much to Skye's
delight. As she took the painting down, Skye knew
it would be loved and appreciated for years to come.*

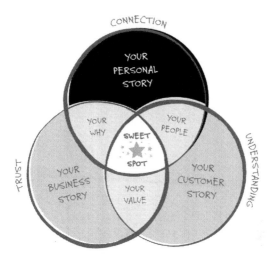

The perfect place to start

Before The Business of Stories existed, when I was supporting and coaching women who were starting their own businesses, I always opened our first call with 'Tell me your story'. It helps that I'm super curious about people, but I soon realised that it's the perfect place to start. Their stories told me so much about them: who they are, where they've been, what's important to them and what they want.

All businesses and brands, no matter how big or small, were started by someone. That someone has a story and that story is fascinating. Whenever I dig into the personal story of a business founder, I find all sorts of hidden gems just waiting to be polished up and brought to life. Even questions that prompt someone to recall a favourite childhood memory can unearth some golden nuggets.

Your own story is one of the most powerful you can share with your audience.

Open mic

In 2017, I was invited to host a Story Stage at the Business Design Centre in London. It was an open mic event and during the day, I heard some incredibly inspiring stories. Some of the people who came up on stage said they'd never told their story to anyone before – but here they were, sharing it with a bunch of strangers.

The energy in the room was high, the attendees were clearly captivated and, as they listened to one another's stories, more and more of them felt compelled to get up and share their own. People were emotional and highly empathetic. Everyone listened intently and many called out words of encouragement and support for the person at the front of the room. Truly meaningful connections were being made, some verbally, some silently.

It was very exciting to watch.

Oxytocin is a feel-good hormone that is released in our bodies when we're sharing and bonding with others. It's present when we feel a sense of belonging, when we feel safe and a part of something

---

> bigger. That's what was happening in that room. People were bonding. Feeling connected. Building trust. If that's not a good reason for sharing stories, I don't know what is.

Your personal story is where you build an emotional *connection* with your audience, and connection is how we as humans survive. In fact, our brains are programmed to do a number of things to ensure we survive and thrive. These include filtering through all the noise to find:

- **Opportunities to bond with others.** We're stronger in tribes, so we don't want to be alone. It's a primal thing. We want to feel like we belong, that we're a valued and appreciated member of the tribe. We want to find our people.

- **Evidence that we're significant.** We want to know that we matter, that we're important, that our life has meaning. At the most basic level, every human wants to feel listened to and understood. Knowing that we matter to others makes us feel secure.

- **Ways to make good decisions.** Good decisions are essential for our survival. In a world full of choices, we need a process for making decisions that are right for us. That process is to look for an emotional charge. We make decisions based on how we feel about something or someone.

What does all that mean for you as you market your business?

Your customers have choices. No matter what you do, there are likely other people who do it too. They might not do it in the same way, they might not even call it the same thing, but whatever you're offering, people could buy something else instead.

To decide who to buy from, your customer will look for who they feel connected to, who makes them feel listened to, understood and important. They will choose the person, business or brand they believe will 'get' them and help them survive and thrive. Storytelling is how you help them make that connection to you.

 Storytelling is one of the most powerful things that connects us as humans.

Your story is inspiring

I am always amazed at how many people have told me my story has inspired them, when at times, I have felt vulnerable sharing it. Think of someone whose story touched you. They will almost certainly have shown some vulnerability.

We all face challenges. We all feel out of our depth sometimes. If talking about what that looks like for you helps someone else, then it is a story worth telling. Believe me, you have a ton of stories about the journey you've been on – the moments you had to dig deep to find the strength, tenacity and resilience to keep going – that will help others feel inspired and more connected to you. When you talk about the challenges you've faced along the way and what got you through the tough times, your audience will feel motivated and encouraged to face theirs.

Whatever level of success you have achieved, whatever mountain you have conquered, it is the story of what it took to get there – the ups and downs, highs and lows – that people will connect with. That's the stuff that makes your story real and relatable. That's what inspires others to believe they too can conquer their own mountain.

I've had clients tell me they think their story is dull because they've never had a major drama or near-death experience. They've never been penniless or homeless, had to save the world, or been abducted by aliens! The problem is, when you've lived your life every day, you might not think there's anything particularly interesting about it. So many times, I've been working with clients and it's been a throwaway remark or quick aside that they barely thought was relevant that has caught my attention.

Here's the thing though: how many people do you know who have a story worthy of a Hollywood movie?

Not many, I bet. Most people have an everyday story just like yours; they aren't looking for someone with a gripping blockbuster because they would struggle to relate to that. In real life, we're all simply looking for people with stories like ours.

Sometimes, it's obvious and easy to see the clear parallels between your story and what will connect with your audience. Maybe you've been exactly where they are right now, facing the same problems and challenges. Other times, it's not so obvious which stories are the right ones to share.

Bumps and bruises

I often talk about the bumps and bruises I've acquired along the way, all of which have been important steps in my journey and made me who I am today. Does the fact that I was a single mum for many years, or risked everything I had by investing it all in property, or suffered from chronic fatigue help me do what I do? Maybe.

The point is, your customers could work with any number of people. When they choose to work with you, it's because there is something about you – your story, your journey, where you've been and what you bring – that helps them feel that, with you in their corner, they could get to where they want to be. If you only talk about your product or service – what it is, how it works and how much it costs – you're not giving people something to connect to and they won't have a compelling reason to choose you.

Uniquely you

There are so many things that make you, you:

- Your accomplishments, experiences, adventures, relationships and travels.

- Lessons you've learned and decisions you've made.

- Life experiences that have shaped you.

- Setbacks that have helped you grow.

- Scars that are a reminder of the obstacles you've overcome.

- Your wisdom, truth, spirit and essence.

- Your perspective, values, ideas and passions.

- Roles you've played and the way you do what you do.

These and many more are all little parts that make up the whole you.

I don't know your story, but I know this: you've lived a life full of experiences. No matter your age or what life has looked like for you so far, your story is packed with fascinating scenes and moments that make it utterly unique. No one else has lived your life. No one else has your story. It's the one thing no one else can copy. It's all yours.

Let's unpack it.

Unpacking your personal story

When my daughter wants to build something with Lego, she first empties her big box of pieces out onto the living room floor. Obviously that means I regularly stand on small abandoned sharp-edged pieces, usually when barefoot with a hot coffee in hand, but I digress.

Before she starts to put any kind of structure or scene together, she lays all the pieces out so she can clearly see what she's got. Unpacking your story is like that. You need to get it all out so you can see what you have to work with.

There are many ways to do that. When I'm working one-to-one with clients, I have lots of questions and prompts to get them talking, while I listen out for the little nuggets and gems. Together we explore territory that, often, they haven't verbalised or even thought about for a long time, if ever. It's always fascinating to see where it takes us and what comes out of their story.

When I'm working with groups and it's not possible to do such focused one-to-one work, I introduce exercises that people can go through together and on their own. Some appeal to the creative members of the group and others are for the more analytical left-brained people who would hate the idea of having to draw anything. I'm going to share some of those exercises throughout this book, and you can find more resources and a companion workbook at www.thebusinessofstories.com/magic.

As you go through the exercises in this chapter, remember that all you are doing here is unpacking. You're not looking to write the perfect narrative yet – there are several more steps before we do that; you're simply bringing thoughts and memories out into the open so you can examine them.

There's no need to be too concerned at this point about whether your stories are relevant or compelling enough. Some might be, some won't be, but you only find little nuggets of gold by sifting through the piles of gravel they sit among.

Without worrying about what story you're going to tell, how you're going to tell it or even who you're going to tell it to, work through these exercises and be curious about what comes up. You don't have to do them all at once. Start with the one that triggers a memory or sparks some ideas. You don't have to do them exactly how I've suggested, either, if you feel compelled to do them another way. These are prompts to help you get started.

Exercise 1: The river of life

This is a great exercise to help you unpack some of the events, moments and scenes that have featured in your life. It is particularly popular with creative people, but you certainly don't need to be an artist to do it. It works best when you use pen and paper or a whiteboard, but go with whatever works for you.

Draw a river running from the top of the piece of paper (or whatever you're using) to the bottom. Remember rivers are full of bends, twists and turns, so let it meander down the paper.

As you think about the journey you've been on, plot some of the significant events that have had an impact and shaped who you are today. Consider:

- Key moments and experiences that have helped form your core values
- Choices and decisions that have led you here
- Hard lessons
- Insights
- Obstacles
- Your achievements, setbacks, pivots and milestones
- People who helped you move forward or held you back

What does your journey look like? What were the turning points?

You can draw shapes, symbols or use key words to represent whatever you want to plot along your River of Life. There are no rules. Have fun with it and see what comes up. If you want to see my example, go to www.thebusinessofstories.com/magic and have a look.

Exercise 2: Life letter

I once did an exercise where I wrote a letter to money. Yep, money. Weird, right? Actually, it was incredibly empowering.

The exercise came from one of my favourite books, *You Are a Badass At Making Money*[3] by *New York Times* bestselling author, success coach and all-round badass Jen Sincero. The idea is that you write a letter to money as if it were a person.

When I saw how powerful the exercise was, I experimented with it in my workshops. I got people to write a letter to themselves when they were a teenager, telling their young self how their own story was going to unfold. Here are the instructions I gave them.

Do this from a place of kindness and compassion. You will have made mistakes along the way, we all do. Talk about the lessons you've learned and how the challenges and hard times have made you who you are today. Write about your successes, achievements, experiences, skills and strengths. Let your younger self get excited about the journey ahead.

This is about getting your story out of your head and on to paper in a way that feels sincere and true to who you are. You can't lie to your younger self, because they're going to find out the truth sooner or later.

3   J Sincero, *You Are a Badass at Making Money: Master the mindset of wealth* (Viking, 2017)

Don't write your letter with your business head on. Just write from your heart and imagine the younger you reading it wide-eyed and open-mouthed, bursting with excitement, pride and gratitude. Tell them the story of their life to date.

Exercise 3: Defining moments

Your life will have had many defining moments. Moments where you had to:

- Step up
- Change
- Walk away or lean in
- Fight for something you believed in
- Ignore the critics
- Overcome a challenge
- Break through a barrier
- Grow into the person you want to be

These are the moments that have defined your life, influenced your decisions and led you down the path you chose to travel. What are some of those moments for you? What did you learn from them? How did they empower you? What changed because of them?

Your fascinating stories are often in your defining moments. Think about what was going on for you and pick one moment that sums up that story. There may have been three or four defining moments on your journey, or there may have been one.

For more exercises to help you unpack your personal story, go to www.thebusinessofstories.com/magic.

At this point, you may have a ton of notes, memories, stories and answers to the questions in this chapter. Alternatively, you may have one story that you feel totally sums up who you are, how you got to where you are now and why it matters. There is no right or wrong. Just go with whatever has come up for you as you've worked through this chapter and any of the online exercises you've completed.

If you haven't made any notes, I highly recommend doing so before you move on. You want to capture your thoughts about your personal story before you turn your attention to your business and customer stories, but remember we're only unpacking at this point. We'll come back to these thoughts and notes later, when we'll be looking at them from the sweet spot in the middle of your Circles of Storytelling Magic. For now, just keep them all together, ready for us to refer to in Chapter 8.

 If you want a place to store them safely you can download the accompanying workbook I've put together for you at www.thebusinessofstories. com/magic.

Congratulations on completing the first step! You're doing a great job.

Storytelling magic

- Our brain is programmed to search for opportunities to connect with others. Sharing your story provides your ideal client with the opportunity to connect with you.

- Now more than ever, we want to feel safe and connected. Storytelling is one of the most powerful things that connects us as humans.

- Oxytocin is a feel-good hormone that is released when we're sharing experiences and bonding with others. Stories bring about chemical changes in the body.

- Your story is unique, the one thing no one else can copy, and fascinating to others.

- People relate to stories that are like theirs, not necessarily the ones worthy of a Hollywood movie.

- If you only talk about your product or service, your customers won't have a compelling reason to choose you.

3

Your Business Story

Treasured possessions

David Wicks had left the corporate world when we worked together in 2017. As we unpacked his story, it became clear that he is passionate about empowering others to reach their full potential. At the heart of everything he does is a belief that talented people should never be overlooked or wasted.

As we chatted about his childhood, I realised where that belief had come from.

'When I was young, my family didn't have a lot,' he told me, 'so we learned to value our possessions and look after them. What we had, we cherished. We didn't replace things when they weren't working properly; we fixed them. They meant something to us and they deserved to be looked after and treasured.'

I had goosebumps. 'David, that's why you're so passionate about nurturing and empowering others. That's why you believe they deserve to be looked after. You don't just value possessions, you value people.'

For the first time, he saw the connection too. That desire to treasure things had stayed with him throughout his life and become the core belief and value to build his business on.

The good, bad and ugly

When did you last share the story of what led you here, doing what you now do? When did you last tell your target market why you chose to do this work? How you found your 'thing'?

How often do you tell people why the work you do matters? Do people know how much it means to you? Why you care? Does your audience understand who you love working with and why, and what a great result you can help them get?

If not, then they don't know. We need to put that right.

But first, I want to clear up something that might be on your mind. I get that your stories are not all sunshine and roses. I understand that not everything you have done in your business has been a success. I know that your journey has been made up of a million little scenes, some of which you may wish had played out differently. Some you may even be embarrassed about.

Here's what I want you to know: everyone's story is like that. No journey is a straight road. No one gets to be successful without collecting some battle scars along the way. We all trip up. Get hit by the curveballs. Try things that don't work. Veer off track. Regret decisions. Feel stupid.

Before you dismiss those stories, think about who they might help. Think about the person who would be inspired to hear that they're not alone and that what they're going through is just part of the journey.

Being vulnerable and sharing the good and bad helps others to feel encouraged about their journey and find the strength to get back up, dust themselves off and carry on. Just like you did.

Building trust

Just as elements of your personal story allow you to create meaningful connections with your audience, your business story helps you build *trust*. When people come across you and your business, they want to feel confident that you're credible and competent, know what you're doing and know how to get them a great result. They want to feel they can trust you with something they don't necessarily trust themselves to do on their own.

Think about this: most people know how to lose weight and get fit, but many will pay coaches to help them because they don't trust themselves to do the things they know they need to do. They want to find someone they feel connected to, someone they believe will help them on the quest they're about to embark on and be there for them, getting them through the ups and downs and helping them keep the vision of what they want their life to look like alive.

How do you show your ideal client that they can trust you? You start by unpacking your business story.

Telling stories is how you put the 'human' into your business and brand.

There will obviously be overlaps with your personal story, but unpacking your business story is about turning the focus to what has led you here, doing the work you now do.

Businesses and brands don't just pop up from nowhere; there's always been a journey. Unpacking that journey helps you see clearly what your origin story is. Like a tree has strong roots to hold it in place, so it can withstand the storms and tensions that might otherwise send it falling to the ground, your origin story gives your business depth and strength.

When customers see that you've been on a journey, that there's a story behind what you do and why you do it, they'll feel they're in good, solid, reliable hands.

The origins of your business might go right back to what you were brought up to believe about money or work or people. They'll almost certainly be based on some core values you formed at an early age that have stayed true to you all your working life. In other words, your origins and core values already exist. They're with you at all times and guide your behaviours and decisions every day. If you're not sure what they are, look no further than your own story.

Stake in the ground

Putting your stake in the ground about what you do is critical if you want clarity, direction and a sound business that has a good chance of growing and thriving. It's about deciding what you want to be known for.

When you don't put a stake in the ground, it's easy to flit from one thing to another, jumping on new business opportunities, constantly trying new tactics and strategies, signing up for more courses, switching from one industry or audience to the next. None of that is going to help you stand strong, tell a clear and coherent story or get known for what you do.

People trust clarity and consistency, so being clear about what you do, who for and why helps you tell a story that builds trust. They want to know that this is your 'thing' and that your work matters to you.

When I hear people talking about the two businesses they run, or the 'hat I'm wearing today', I want to tell them they've just massively diluted their message. The story immediately feels complicated, disjointed.

Great stories have one strong storyline, and you know immediately what it is. Dorothy needs to get back home to Kansas. Marlin needs to find Nemo. Rocky wants to beat his opponent and be a world champion.

Unpacking your business story can help you define your one storyline and put your stake in the ground.

Moments of insight

Life is full of 'aha' moments of insight. Just as we looked at defining moments in your personal story, you will have had many moments on this business journey of yours that influenced and determined the direction you took. Maybe you had an 'aha' moment about your work that lit you up so much, it's never felt like work. Maybe the things you find easy, other people find challenging. Maybe you can see a solution where others are struggling to find an answer.

British mum Cara Sayer invented the SnoozeShade, a sort of blackout blind for prams, because she was fed up with hanging blankets and coats over her pram so that her daughter could sleep. When she noticed how many other mums were doing the same, she realised it was a problem that needed a resolution.

Sara Blakely cut the feet out of a pair of control-top tights and wore them under her new cream trousers because she didn't want visible panty lines – and she wanted to look thinner. They weren't great and rolled up her legs all night, but she knew she was on to something. Her multimillion-dollar company Spanx was born.

Unpacking your moments of insight, and what action you took as a result of having them, can show others what makes you tick and what matters to you in your work. Like all your stories, your business journey is unique to you. No one else has had the same journey. No one else has experienced the challenges and struggles you have in exactly the same way. The path you alone have trodden is full of fascinating stories.

Over the years, I've helped craft stories about childhoods rich in experiences, art, culture and travel, experiences that ignited a passion or sparked an idea that became a theme for someone's life. Experiences like those of the print designer whose love of clothes came from going to jumble sales as a child with her Nana Pat; or the interior designer who built a treehouse in a tree, inside her home; or the photographer whose passion was sparked the first time he saw an image emerge in a darkroom.

Your stories are fascinating to others because they haven't lived your life. Your journey helps others to join the dots and see what passion, experiences and stories you bring to your work. That's how you differentiate. That's how you stand out from the crowd. *You* are your unique selling proposition (USP) and you have a great story.

Survival instincts

It was Maxine's turn to do her sixty-second pitch. She talked about her one-stop party shop with 'all the supplies you need under one roof' and 'banners and balloons to make your party go with a bang'. She knew her pitch well, she'd recited it so many times, and this was speed-networking so, in a few minutes, she was going to say it all over again at the next table.

Then she heard me talk about storytelling and it got her thinking. At the next table, she didn't do her usual pitch. Instead, she shared her story.

She talked about how she had become a single mum in 2011, labelled 'unemployable' after her violent ex had inflicted back injuries that meant she couldn't sit or stand for long periods of time. She shared how her survival instincts had kicked in. Determined not to be beaten anymore, she vowed to do something for herself and her two young children.

She wrote a business plan and, over the last few years, had put her heart and soul into bringing that business to life.

Everyone at the table listened intently. They were completely engrossed in her story, clearly moved and inspired, and when she finished, they asked for her business card.

People want a reason to buy from you. Your story is that reason.

Unpacking your business story

There are all sorts of ways to unpack your business story. Here are a few suggestions that will help you join up the dots and see the mountain of stories and value you're sitting on. They'll help you recognise the things that make you and your business unique, that set you apart from everybody else, and that will ultimately move you away from being a commodity and having to compete on price (more about that in Chapter 7).

Work through the exercises below, but also think about talking to some of the people you work with – your virtual assistant, coach, bookkeeper, or even previous clients if you feel comfortable doing so. Getting another perspective can be super helpful. When you're so close to what you do, it can be hard to see yourself the way others do.

Exercise 1: Core belief

What's the core belief that underpins everything you do? It's a question I always pose to clients, but they've rarely truly thought about it before I ask. There will be one. It's why your business exists.

Here are some famous examples:

- IKEA believes homes should be a perfect reflection of the people who live inside them.
- TOMS® Shoes believe they can improve people's lives through business.
- Starbucks believes a coffeehouse should be a place to find moments of connection.
- Nike believes anyone can be an athlete.

If you're not sure what your core belief is, put 'I believe...' at the top of a piece of paper and just start writing whatever comes to mind. Let your thoughts flow. Don't strive for one perfect answer or be critical or keep editing.

Then dig a little deeper. Ask yourself why you believe that. Why is that important?

Aim for ten beliefs and notice if there is a 'theme' emerging. Maybe you've said the same thing several different ways.

You'll know you've unpacked your one core belief when it feels true and congruent. When it excites you. When it feels like it encapsulates everything your business stands for.

Exercise 2: The road to here

Think about the business journey you've been on. You may have unpacked some of this in the River of Life exercise, but now think specifically about how you have ended up here, doing the work you do.

- What does that journey look like?
- What business successes and failures have you had along the way?
- What events or people have been significant, good or bad?
- What challenges have you had to overcome?
- What has been your proudest moment so far?

Think about the lessons you've learned and how those learnings have shaped your business journey.

Write about your road to here.

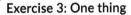

Exercise 3: One thing

So many business owners struggle to focus on one thing, yet look behind any story of extraordinary success and you will find the power of one thing in play:

- Tetley does tea.
- KFC does chicken.
- Google does search.
- Levi's does jeans.
- Xero does accounting software.
- Green & Blacks does chocolate.
- Five Guys does burgers.

When you focus on and get known for one thing, it's far more likely people will remember what you do. It'll be easier for people to talk about you, and you'll stand out in a sea of other businesses who are too afraid to commit to one thing.

What's your one thing?

Exercise 4: One word

What one word sums up what your business – and brand – is about? Just one word. Take some time to think about it.

Answers I've heard from clients over the years include:

- Fun, adventure, rebel.
- Bold, pioneering, innovation.
- Truth, flow, peace.

Can you guess what my one word is? There are a few words it could be – connection, clarity, communication – but when I really thought about it, I decided it was curiosity. (No idea why all my words begin with C!) To deeply connect with the people I want to work with, I need to start by getting curious. For me, everything starts with curiosity.

What about you?

Once you have your one word, think about how it shows up in your business and what stories are aligned with it. What stories could you tell that would help others see that that's what your business stands for?

Distilling the problem you solve and how you make people's lives better down to one word can help inform your messaging and stories moving forward.

For more exercises to help you unpack your business story, go to www.thebusinessofstories.com/magic.

Make sure you capture the thoughts and ideas that have come up as you've worked through this chapter and any of the online exercises you've completed before you turn your attention to your customer story.

Keep all your notes together in your workbook, ready to work with when we look at them again from the sweet spot of your Circles of Storytelling Magic.

We'll come back to them in Part Three, when you'll be ready to craft and share them.

Good job! You're doing great.

 ## Storytelling magic

- People buy from people they know, like and trust. Your business story helps you build that trust.

- Businesses and brands don't appear from nowhere. There's been a journey and unpacking that helps you tell your origin story.

- Putting your stake in the ground helps you stand strong, tell a clear and coherent story and get known for what you do.

- The path you alone have trodden is full of fascinating stories. You are your USP.

- There is a core belief and set of values behind what you do. Telling your story is how you humanise your brand.

- Behind any story of extraordinary success, you will find the power of one thing in play.

4

Your Customer Story

The dressmaker

Vee Tanner wanted to turn her lifelong love of dress-making into a business. She wanted to make dresses and outfits for female entrepreneurs and business leaders who spend a lot of time on stage or presenting to groups and whose appearance is important to them. The way they present themselves is a big part of their personal brand and their clothes need to fit the image they want to convey.

Vee was keen for her key message to focus on the sustainability of the materials she used. Sustainability is an important topic, and she was sure her audience would want to know that she used ethically sourced materials.

However, a survey in a Facebook group full of her target market showed that her message needed to focus on something different. The top three things this group of female speakers wanted were outfits that were super comfortable to wear, that flattered their shape and made them feel confident all day. It wasn't that ethically sourced materials weren't of interest; it just wasn't the most important thing, so wasn't the story that would grab Vee's audience's attention the moment they landed on her site.

'Bespoke dresses that look beautiful, fit like a glove and feel authentically you' was.

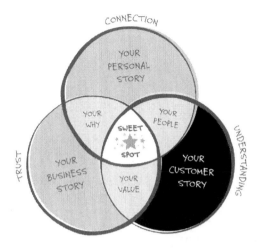

What do they want?

Telling your customer story is how you show that you *understand* them; that you totally get what's going on for them.

When I talk about your customer story, I'm not talking about the usual demographic data that a lot of marketers focus on. To be honest, I've never really found knowing what newspaper my customer reads, how many children they have or where they shop to be particularly helpful. When putting your customer story together, you're looking for the thing they *all* want.

You may be a therapist who can help people with everything from phobias and exam stress to weight loss and addictions, but what do all of those people want that's the same:

- For life to be easier?
- To change the story they're running in their head?
- To have support so they no longer have to struggle alone?

You're looking for an overarching theme: a storyline that is true for *all* of them. All your clients are different, but you're looking for the things they have in common, related to what you do. Unpacking your customer story starts with understanding what they're all struggling with right now and what story they're telling themselves about what they can and can't do.

Who buys physio?

When I worked with Vanbrugh Physio, one of the largest and best-known physio clinics in South London, I spent time interviewing several of the company's clients to capture the language they were using to describe the problem they had and the solution they were looking for.

As I went through the transcripts of the interviews, one particular phrase came up again and again: 'I just want to get back to...'

What they wanted to get back to was different for each person. Some wanted to get back to the gym or the sport they loved. Some wanted to be able to spend hours pottering around in their garden, like they used to. One mother wanted to be able to pick her toddler up again without experiencing pain. A sixty-three-year-old man wanted to go back to playing hockey. Another elderly man had spent 80% of the last sixteen years lying on a hard floor, trying to get some relief from severe back pain. Sixteen years! He wanted to get back to living a normal life – standing up.

Despite their stories all being different, there was a clear theme to them all. These people *all* wanted to get back to doing the things they love and living life to the full.

That was the story Vanbrugh Physio needed to be telling.

There is a ton of value in speaking to your customers – because they will often describe the problem differently to the way you do. And there's a simple explanation for that.

As a business owner, you've likely been doing what you do for a few years. Over time, you'll have come to think about it in a certain way. Whether you're aware of it or not, you've probably adopted words and phrases that you use all the time and settled on a particular way of talking about what you do, who you do it for and what problem you solve. It may have been a while since you checked in and made sure that the language you're so familiar with is the language your target market uses and will resonate with.

I've found that my client's clients often summarise what my client helped them do, what problem they solved and what result they got in a far better, simpler way than my client could.

Pure Gold

When I worked with business coach Dino Tartaglia, he knew his target market well. He was also aware that the language he was using was not landing the way he wanted it to with the clients he wanted to attract.

He talked about how he helped clients organise their thoughts, simplify their business and grow their income. He talked about how his clients wanted freedom but needed structure, and how they often ended up going in the wrong direction until they ran out of steam or burnt out. He talked about what he could help his clients with using analogies and metaphors about fishes, water, nature reserves and electric fences. He talked about knowing what they needed to do and how to help them, but he didn't know how to engage them with a clear message and a story they could relate to that would compel them to take action.

As we worked together, I encouraged him to get feedback from his clients and send it to me. As I read through the responses, I found some pure gold in there, including these magic words:

'Dino helps you build a business around being brilliant at what you do.'

There it was. Clear and simple.

In just a few words, Dino's client had summed up what he does and who for: people who are brilliant at what they do, but don't know how to build a business doing it. How he helps them is the detail he could fill in later. Understanding their brilliance, and building a business around it, is what his ideal clients all want, and it formed the theme of an exciting story he could invite them in to.

Understanding the journey

It's important to know the journey your ideal customer is on, where they are right now, where they've been and where they want to go.

Understanding how long they've been trying to solve the problem they have, what other solutions they've tried and how urgent it is for them, will help you see where you fit into their story.

A new parent, for instance, is going to be suddenly faced with a whole set of challenges they've not encountered before. It's an exciting, chaotic and often scary time – and one they'll want to feel they're 'mastering' as soon as possible. Any problems that arise they'll want to be on top of quickly, so they can keep their little one safe and be the calm and confident parent they want to be. When they look for help, they'll want to trust that the people and brands they buy in to can guide them to navigate this new journey successfully, so they feel in safe and experienced hands.

Someone who has put up with lying on a hard floor for 80% of the last sixteen years because of back pain has probably given up hope. It's an old story they've likely accepted they're not going to be able to change. They may be cautious and weary about new treatments, getting their hopes up or believing that someone has the magic pill. Before they try anything else, they'll need to believe it's worth investing more time, money and energy in, and that someone can help where so many others have failed.

The what-ifs

Talking about what will happen if your customer doesn't solve the problem you can help them solve is another important part of your customer story. I'm sure you've heard about the overworked, stressed-out CEO who finally shifted the extra weight he'd been carrying, focused on getting fitter and made some important life changes – *after* a mild heart attack and sobering warning from his doctor. The frazzled and exhausted consultant and mother who finally started to delegate and build a strong support team around her, both at work and at home – *after* she found herself so burnt out from trying to do it all on her own, she could barely function. The media company founder who finally got a robust cybersecurity and disaster recovery plan in place – *after* they experienced a cyber-attack that threatened to damage the reputation they'd worked hard for years to build.

For people to act, there must be something at stake. Otherwise, they won't be motivated enough to put in the effort to do what needs to be done. Unpacking your customer story helps you identify if they're likely to be looking for help before the problem grows, or after it has shown up and hit them smack-bang in the face.

Talking about the consequences you can help your customer avoid, even if those consequences are that nothing changes, needs to be a part of the story you're telling.

Feel the fear

It's also important to tune into any fear your customer may be feeling. If they haven't found the happy ever after to their story yet, it means something's in the way. They may know exactly what's in the way, but not how to get past it. Alternatively, they may not know what it is; they just know that something is stopping them from living the life they want.

You need to understand this part of your customer story like no other – where they're at, how they're feeling, what the challenge is and what's stopping them from showing up the way they want to.

People will buy from you when they believe you can help them move on, make things happen, change the current story and live the life they want to be living. You need to know the story they're telling themselves and the fear that's holding them back. Showing that you understand that will set you apart from those just trying to sell a product or service.

 Telling your customer story is how you show that you understand them.

Unpacking your customer story

There are many ways to unpack your customer story. You'll always get the best information and insight from talking to your customers and capturing their thoughts and language, so look for every opportunity to do that.

Here are a few exercises to get you started.

Exercise 1: The commonalities

Look for the commonalities in your customers' stories. Of course, they will all have a unique story, but there will be a theme around whatever it is that your business exists to help them with.

Think about the clients you've worked with. What did they all want? Identifying that helps you pan out and see the overarching story that is relevant for all of them.

You may be able to help all sorts of people with all sorts of problems, but what do all your clients have in common? What do they all want?

Exercise 2: The genie

If you could hand your ideal client a magic lamp and all they had to do was rub it and a genie would appear and grant them one wish, what would they wish for? What is the one thing that would make the biggest difference for them in their life, business, health or whatever it is that you can help them with? Obviously, it needs to be related to the product or service you provide.

In other words, what's their 'If only...'?

Exercise 3: Ask the audience

The first time I talk to a prospect or run any kind of discovery call, I'm looking to find out what's going on for them, where they're at, what problem they want to solve and what might be in the way. Talking to your customers is the best way to unpack your customer story.

This can be done many ways, including interviewing them, asking previous clients for feedback, sending out a survey or simply conducting a poll in an online group full of your target market. Get good at asking questions and listening to the responses.

Questions like:

- What is your biggest challenge and why do you think it's such a challenge?
- How is it making you feel?
- What do you think might be in the way of you getting that problem sorted?
- What solutions have you tried and what results did you see?
- What's made you take action now?
- In a perfect world, what would be available to solve that problem?
- What difference will it make when that challenge is no longer a problem for you?
- How will that feel?

Obviously, you'll want to make those questions relevant to what you do, but the people who are coming to you, looking for help to solve a problem, will help you put a pretty accurate and insightful customer story together.

If your business involves you getting on the phone with a prospect or doing any kind of discovery call, make sure (with their permission) you record the calls so you can go back and capture their language. If you have an opportunity to get feedback from clients after you've worked with them, do that too.

For examples, exercises and a workbook that will help you unpack your customer story, go to www. thebusinessofstories.com/magic

Make sure you capture the thoughts and ideas that have come up as you've worked through this chapter and any of the online exercises before you turn your attention to Part Two – Explore.

You're doing great. Nice work so far!

 Storytelling magic

- Unpacking and telling your customer story is how you show that you truly and deeply understand them.

- Listen to what your customers are saying. This is the best way to capture the language they use when talking about what they want and what's in the way of them having that.

- Identifying the thing that all your customers want will help you tell a story that is simple but compelling.

- To understand where you fit in your customer's story, you first need to understand where they are in their journey, how long they've been trying to solve their problem and what else they've tried.

- Something is holding your customer back from having what they want. Unpacking what that is will give your customer story depth and power.

PART TWO: EXPLORE

Exploring your stories to find purpose, meaning and connection

5
Your Why

Brain damage

If you'd met Sherry Bevan in 1987, you'd have seen an ambitious woman. Her corporate career had started in information technology (IT) at a large accountancy firm where she spent eleven years working her way up.

On the outside, she looked extremely successful, but success at work was coming at a cost. She knew she wasn't getting the work/life balance right. There was no balance.

Desperate to find ways to 'switch off' from work, she took up cycling – but approached that with the same high-energy determination and ambition she approached everything else. A couple of racing accidents later, she had a broken leg and brain damage.

Not one to be beaten, she recovered quickly, but continued 'full-speed' through life, until the years of not taking care of herself took their toll. She was constantly feeling overwhelmed and suffered from irritable bowel syndrome. When she found herself wanting to self-harm, she knew something had to change so she changed jobs, but her corporate career continued for another thirteen years.

Finally, determined not to miss out on seeing her two daughters grow up, Sherry decided to leave the corporate world once and for all. She took a deep breath and a big leap of faith, quit her highly paid IT job and set up her own coaching business. The Confident Mother conference, book, podcast and coaching programme was born.

Sherry's 'why' jumps out of her story. She focuses on helping smart, ambitious women in tech and the professional services recognise their own value, innate talents and strengths – because she knows only too well those are the things they often struggle to see in themselves.

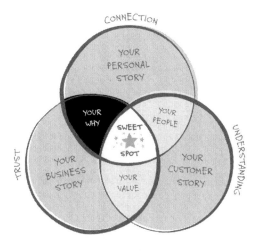

Two whys

Now that you've spent time reflecting on your journey and unpacking your personal, business and customer stories, we're going to look at what lies in the intersections between them. This is where you can dig a little deeper into why you do what you do, who you want to do it for and what value you provide.

 We are happiest when doing work that feels meaningful to us. Customers will get the best of us when our work is fulfilling.

Between your personal story and your business story is your *why*: the bridge that connects the journey you've been on, the experiences you've had, the person you are today and the business you gave birth to and brought into the world.

Let's explore that.

I struggled with knowing what my 'why' was for many years. If I'm honest, it used to irritate me when people asked me what it was. I worried that I was shallow because I didn't have a big, bold, socially conscious goal of wanting to change the world. I didn't really have a why at all; I just liked doing work I was good at that made me happy, got great results for my clients and that I got paid well for doing.

Like millions of other people, I read Simon Sinek's *Start With Why*,[4] and then went round and round in circles for a long time, trying to find a why that was 'good enough'. But I couldn't. Was that bad?

Then I heard a coach in the United States describe the whole why thing slightly differently and it totally re-framed it for me, made a lot of sense and took the pressure I'd been feeling off. I now talk about how we have two whys.

Firstly, there's your 'why you do what you do'. There may be all sorts of reasons for this. Perhaps you want to work for yourself, you don't want to be tied to one location, or you don't want anyone else telling you

---

4   S Sinek, *Start With Why: How great leaders inspire everyone to take action* (Penguin, 2011)

what time you have to start or when you can have a day off. Maybe you decided to turn your love for doing something into a living, or you saw a gap in the market and a business opportunity just sitting there waiting to be grabbed. Your 'why you do what you do' is for you.

Then there's your big why. Your big why is what's compelling to others. It's the difference you make, even if it's only to a handful of people. It's what you want for the people you love to work with. It has purpose, meaning, emotion. It's more than what you make; it's what you make happen.

You might not feel like you're changing the world but you are, in some way, making it better for the people you serve. As Pat Flynn says in his book *Superfans*, 'You don't need to change the entire world to build a successful business; you just need to change someone's world.'[5]

Whether you're helping smart, ambitious women recognise their own worth, innate skills and strengths, or making sure talent is valued, not wasted, people will be drawn to your big why. When I'm working with clients, I rarely have to ask them their big why. I see it. I feel it. I hear it when they share their stories with me.

---

5   P Flynn, *Superfans: The easy way to stand out, grow your tribe, and build a successful business* (Get Smart Books, 2019)

It only takes a moment

In a busy craft market in Salisbury, one stall stood out. Stylish black boxes with a striking black-and-gold branding were expertly displayed, brimming with beautiful thoughtfully selected products. A sign on the table simply read: 'It only takes a moment to create a moment'.

As I browsed the stall, the young couple who stood behind it with their son told me the story behind those words.

'A couple of years ago, we found ourselves going through some really tough stuff as a family – both personally and professionally. We did come out the other side, but when we looked back and thought about how we got through it, we realised it was the little moments that kept us all going: the smiles, the hugs, the gestures. A cup of tea, a foot rub, a note or a few kind words of encouragement.

'We realised we could handle the big stuff that was going on because those little moments gave us all the support and strength we needed to get through it together. We wanted to create something so others could appreciate and celebrate their own little moments. Our gift boxes help people make any day special by showing love and appreciation to those around them.'

And there it was: the big why that lived between their personal story and their business story, wrapped up in beautiful branding and simply told.

Storytelling is a two-way experience. It's a co-creation between the person sharing it and the person engaging with it. In fact, people are only half listening to *your* story because, at the same time, they're thinking about *their* story.

That couple in Salisbury had a powerful story that gave meaning and purpose to what was otherwise a table of beautiful gift boxes, but the message wrapped up inside it went even deeper for me. As they were talking about their little moments, I looked across to where my husband and daughter were standing at another stall and felt an overwhelming sense of gratitude for their love and support. I felt quite emotional, thinking about how we as a family are there for each other, but maybe, we don't always take the time to appreciate the special everyday moments that give us all the strength to take on whatever life throws at us.

Hearing that couple's story triggered my brain to look for ways in which it had meaning for me, personally. It made me reflect on my life and how grateful I am for the people in it. It connected with me emotionally; their big why resonated with me deeply. I got it. I felt it.

Did I buy something from their stall? Yes, I did. Then I went home and looked at their website and bought something else. I wrote a blog about them and since that day, I've told countless other people about them.

If you make jewellery or cakes or websites or coffee machines and think this doesn't apply to you, let me tell you that the only difference between that couple and every other stallholder in the market that day was that they told me their story. That's the magic of storytelling.

The science of why

'People don't buy *what* you do, they buy *why* you do it' has become more than a message. It's become a movement.

Here's the science behind it. When we talk about what we do, we're using the outer section of our brain, the neocortex, which is responsible for analytical thinking and language. Whereas, when we talk about why we do something, we're activating the middle section of our brain, the limbic system, which is responsible for our behaviour, decision making and feelings.

As I mentioned in Chapter 2, we make decisions based on how we're feeling. You've likely heard it said that people buy on emotion and justify with logic. We make decisions first with our heart, then with our head. Your customers will make decisions based on how they *feel* about you, your brand, your message and your story.

One of the most powerful emotions you can evoke among your target market is hope.

As humans, we follow brands that give us hope. Hope that we'll be safer, calmer, happier, healthier, wealthier, more confident, more successful. Explaining what you do isn't going to evoke an emotion. Explaining why you do what you do will.

Think about how you feel when someone says, 'I'm a leadership coach.' Now compare that to, 'I believe talented people should never be wasted. They should be nurtured, valued and encouraged to reach their full potential. I work with leaders to help them embrace their strengths, play full in and lead with confidence.' Which one makes you feel something?

Think about the brands that tell you their why. Nike believes anyone can be an athlete. So much more compelling than 'We sell trainers'.

From A to B

Something happened in 2004 that changed the world forever. Facebook happened. The launch of Facebook, and YouTube a year later, meant people were able to connect and share stories with other people around the world, 24/7.

As a result, the way business is done changed. We moved away from it being transactional, ie 'This is what we do, this is what it costs, here's why you should buy it', to being about building relationships first.

This forced companies to think about their big why as they saw that consumers wanted to connect first, get to know a brand, get a sense of what it's about and what it stands for. They wanted to be listened to and understood, not just sold to.

Emirates Airline was quick to spot this global shift towards connection and changed its messaging from 'Taking people from A to B' to 'Connecting people around the world'. A subtle shift, but an important one.

Southwest Airlines started sharing 'The stories behind every seat' and talking about its big why: helping people embark on life adventures and meaningful experiences. They realised they were not in the business of flying planes; they were in the business of flying people.

Exploring your why

There are many ways to explore your big why. Over the years, I've collected and curated several exercises to spark ideas and get you thinking about the multitude of stories you have. There will be overlaps and not every exercise in this book is going to give you a different story, but they are all designed to help you explore your stories in different ways.

Here are some of the exercises that have helped my clients explore their big why.

Exercise 1: A movement

A movement is something that's way bigger than you. It's bigger than your business and the work you do daily. It's a rally cry. It's about the impact you want to make, the difference you want to see in the world.

The thing with a movement is that if people connect with the purpose or cause behind it, they'll feel compelled to join it. They'll want to be a part of it because it's something bigger than they could ever achieve on their own.

Think about some of the movements in history:

- Gay rights, animal rights, civil rights
- Hippies, free love
- Black Lives Matter
- Me Too
- Veganism

Movements aren't about selling things. They generate an energy that picks up momentum and inspires people to create the world they want to see.

If your business was a movement, what would that movement be?

Exercise 2: Dear business

When Kobe Bryant announced his retirement from basketball in 2016, he did so with a poem entitled Dear Basketball.[6] Essentially, it was a love letter to the sport that had been a huge passion and important part of his life since he was a six-year-old boy.

Close your eyes and take yourself forward to the last day of working in your business. Smile as you look back over the years and feel a real sense of having made a difference.

What would you want to say to your business? How would you put into words how you feel about what it gave you and other people? How it brought you joy and helped you make a difference in people's lives?

Kobe's poem conveys love, passion and gratitude for the sport he was leaving behind. Write a letter to your business from your heart. Your big why will be in that letter.

Exercise 3: Making an impact

The work you do makes a difference because it solves a problem. Whatever that problem is, by solving it, you are enabling your customer to move on, achieve success and get the happy ever after they're looking for.

---

6   'Dear Basketball': https://dearbasketball.com

Think about how you inspire and enable them to do that. Now think about stories that work best to get across what that looks and feels like – for you and your customer. Stories about why you do what you do convey the essence of who you are at your best and the impact you make when you do the work you love and care about most.

Your customers will get the best of you when the work you do feels meaningful to you. Whatever you do, whether it's coach, consult, cook, build websites, design interiors, teach golf or give financial advice, people will feel if you're passionate about it.

What is it about your work and serving others that makes you feel fulfilled? What do you enable and inspire others to do, be and have? How are you making the world a little bit better for someone today?

There's your big why.

 Go to www.thebusinessofstories.com/magic for more exercises and a workbook to help you explore your why.

Make sure you capture the thoughts and ideas that have come up as you've worked through this chapter and any of the online exercises you've completed before you move on to exploring your people.

You're making great progress.

Storytelling magic

- Between your personal story and your business story is your *why*. It's the journey you've been on, the person you are today, the business you brought into the world and the impact you make.

- You have two whys: your own personal why you do what you do and your big why. Your big why is more than what you do or what you make; it's what you make happen.

- Storytelling is a two-way thing. When we talk about a story resonating with someone, it means they get it. They know it. They feel it too.

- Explaining what you do speaks to the analytical thinking part of your customer's brain, not the emotional and decision-making part. People buy something because of how it makes them feel.

- Business has moved away from being transactional. People want to be listened to and understood, not just sold to.

6
Your People

I panicked

When a friend asked me why I had started a group for women in business back in 2015, I found myself telling her my story. I talked about becoming a single mum on my daughter's sixth birthday, when her father and I finally decided to part ways. How I'd worked ridiculously long hours, taking all the work I could get to keep our house, a decent lifestyle and everything together for my daughter. How I'd finally burnt out, struggled with chronic fatigue and spent years desperately trying to get my health, life and mojo back on track.

I told her how I had worked hard to build up a buy-to-let property portfolio so I could feel confident about our future, only to fall into a deep personal financial crisis when the housing market crashed.

How I met my husband in 2006 and left the big city a couple of years later with my then teenage daughter to become a London-girl-turned-farmer's-wife. I talked about discovering something called The Lightning Process,[7] finally sorting my chronic fatigue and feeling called to start a community to help women find the support they need to succeed in business, all at the same time as having another daughter in my forties.

'You need to tell that story,' she said. 'People will relate to it and understand where you've come from and why this work matters to you.'

So, that's exactly what I did. I have to say hitting the button to send my story out to 1,500 or so women in business was an incredibly uncomfortable experience.

What if no one reads it? What if no one cares? Why should they?

I was feeling quite sick with panic until, about twenty minutes later, an email popped into my inbox. Reading it made me emotional. It was from someone thanking me for my honesty and saying how inspired they were by my story.

A couple of minutes later I got another one, from someone who had been a member of my group for

---

7   P Parker, 'The Lightning Process', https://lightningprocess.com

months, but only now, after reading my story, felt compelled to get in touch. She told me how much she related to my journey and thanked me for being so open.

And so it continued. For days!

So many women contacted me to say they resonated with my story and how moving and inspiring they had found it. Showing my vulnerability and my personal struggles had made me more 'human'. It meant people could relate to me. I was no longer just a name on a website or a moderator of a group.

People continued to email me. My group sprang to life as members engaged with me and the rest of the group. The enquiries kept coming in and my coaching slots filled up.

I had found my people.

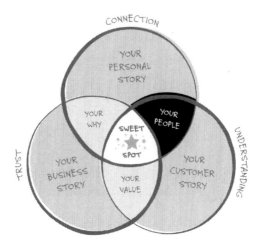

Proposition and purpose

You've already unpacked your personal story and your customer story. In The Circles of Storytelling Magic, your *people* lie between the two. This is where you can go deeper into who your ideal client is: the person you feel most called to serve and can make the biggest difference to.

Let's explore that.

As we've worked together, I've had clients narrow their target market down and gain a deeper understanding of their own motivations, proposition and purpose. Unpacking and exploring your stories can help you focus on a niche and an ideal client.

For instance, if you are a therapist, when you were unpacking your customer story, you may have identified that anxiety is getting in the way of your customers having the life they want. They constantly feel overwhelmed and don't know where to turn for help. That's a problem you can help them with.

However, thinking now about your own journey, you may realise the work that truly lights you up the most and where you can make the biggest difference is working with parents who are struggling to scale their own business and be there for their young children. They feel totally overwhelmed, and it's a story you can deeply relate to because you've been there too.

The link between your story and your customer story is a powerful one. It's where you will find your people.

I totally get any reluctance you may be feeling towards narrowing down your target market too much. It can seem counterintuitive, especially if your business is fairly new or you're not getting as many clients as you'd like. Why would you want to make your target market smaller or say anything that could put people off? The last thing you want is to have potential customers thinking that what you offer is not for them, right?

Here's the thing I've found over and over again. The more specific you are about the people you want to work with, the more your message will cut through the noise and be heard by those people, and the more enquiries you'll get. It's true!

Think of it this way. If you were a fisherman and you wanted to catch a prize carp, you would buy equipment specifically designed to catch carp, and fish in waters that you know are full of them. You'd use bait you know the carp love; you'd use the right size hook, rod and net; you'd do everything you could to set yourself up for success. What you wouldn't do is throw any old rod, hook and bait out into a random river, hoping that you'd somehow catch the exact fish you want.

When it comes to exploring the people part of your Circles of Storytelling Magic, you don't want to be random or have a wide-open net. Getting clear on who your people are will help you craft a message and share stories that will attract the very clients you want to work with.

The power of specificity

I recently heard a coach say that she worked with 'women aged twenty-eight to thirty who have just been promoted into their first leadership role'. That's specific, and there's power in that because it allows for three things to happen:

- **You get a deep understanding of your target market.** That coach clearly knew her audience well. She understood where they were on their journey and what support they needed, right now. As a result, she could create highly tailored coaching programmes and provide the support that she knew would get those specific women a great result.

- **Your messaging speaks directly to your audience.** Trying to connect with everyone is hard; speaking to a specific audience about their pain, fears, wants and desires is powerful. Prospects are never going to be left wondering if you're a good fit for them when you clearly understand them so well and are sharing stories that deeply resonate with them and where they're at.

- **People talk about you to other people.** Being specific about your target market makes it easy for others to talk about you. When someone tells you their area of expertise is 'leadership coaching' you're unlikely to tell others because it's just too broad, but when someone tells you they work with women aged twenty-eight to thirty who have recently been promoted into their first leadership role, you're far more likely to recommend them to people you know in that specific target market.

The tale of two Garys

Gary Belkin's business was two years old, but his workflow wasn't consistent, and he couldn't take on any staff as he didn't feel confident there was enough work in the pipeline to justify it. He wrote a blog and posted on social media but didn't get much engagement.

How come? Because he didn't want to niche or focus on a specific ideal client for fear of putting others off, so he simply talked about his 'financial services'. His messaging was generic and his topics broad; he didn't stand out and he wasn't memorable.

Gary Das's business was also a couple of years old but gaining real traction, and he was getting famous for what he did. His consultancy was busy and he was building a team. His book, *The Self-Employed Mortgage Guide*,[8] had got to number one on Amazon and he was being invited to speak on stages at huge events, full of his target market.

How come? Because he knew who his people were – self-employed people who needed a mortgage. That's it. That's all he talked about, and his story and messaging spoke directly to his target market. It was super easy for people to tell others what he did and who for, so news spread.

---

8   G Das, *The Self-Employed Mortgage Guide: The key to buying any property* (Rethink Press, 2019)

That's the reality. The more specific you are about what you do and who for, the more likely it is that person will hear about it and show up.

The value of focus

Focusing on a specific customer makes it much easier for those customers to say yes.

Imagine you've written a book and you are looking for help to promote and launch it on all your social-media channels. You've asked in a couple of groups and four social-media experts have been recommended to you. You check out their websites and they're all clearly experienced and knowledgeable.

Three of them have a long list of things they can help you with on all things social media. The fourth specialises in book launches. In fact, it's all they do, and their website is full of stories about the successful book launches they've helped their clients with and testimonials from happy authors.

Which one would you want to work with? It's a no-brainer, right?

What if the book-launch social-media consultant was more expensive than the others? Would you be willing to pay a bit more to feel confident that you're in expert, experienced and highly capable hands? I'm guessing you would.

That is the beauty of focusing on your people. The more specific the problem you solve, the more specific the audience you serve, the more your products and services will be respected and valued. Trying to be all things to all people doesn't work anywhere near as well. It weakens your offer, decreases your value and makes it almost impossible to stand out.

 Specialising makes what you do 'special' and special is worth more.

Removing the fear

If you're not sure who you make the biggest difference to, start asking the questions that will help you find out.

Whenever I finish working with a client, I ask them four questions. I'll go through all four questions in Chapter 10, but one is 'What do you now have as a result of working with me and what difference has that made to you and your business?'

The answers I've had back from clients over the years have really helped me see the impact my work is having and who I'm making the biggest difference to.

They've also given me tons of stories I can then share if I want to attract similar clients and work.

Marion Ellis, the founder of Love Surveying, answered that question by telling me about her biggest fear. 'I couldn't articulate my new niche and brand the way I wanted to. It was affecting my confidence and belief that it was even a "thing". The clarity and confidence I now have to explain what I do and how I do it have taken away the fear I was feeling. I've already had new clients reach out and new opportunities open up, so yes, it is a thing.'

Did I want to work with more clients like Marion? Yes, I did. Did I start talking about how getting your stories right can help you gain clarity and confidence, and take away any fear you have that what you do is even a 'thing'? Yes, I did.

Not an agency

Ben Davis and Simon Batchelar are digital marketing experts who had been down the 'agency' route.

They'd had the big teams and the big clients. They'd experienced what it was like to be juggling multiple projects and accounts, and they didn't want to do it anymore. They didn't feel as connected to the work or the clients as they had when there was just the two of them, so they downsized the agency, got clear on who they wanted to work with and went back to doing the work they loved.

They knew they would lose the clients who wanted to work with big agencies and that was OK. These clients were no longer a good fit for them. They removed the layers of project managers and account executives and were excited to work closely with small business owners who were scaling to reach their first £1 million in revenue. Working personally on every project and speaking to every client, they got to know their customers well and enjoyed celebrating every success with them.

When we worked together in 2016, we shared the story they knew their people would connect with. 'We're not a big corporate digital agency. We've been there and it's not what we're about. We're two guys who love what we do and get excited about what our clients are doing.'

They got clear on who they wanted to work with, stopped trying to be bigger and focused on being better at the work that lights them up. They focused on their people.

Exploring your people

Exercise 1: Your people

Think about the person you feel most called to serve.

Who is the person you want to help win? Who is the person you can deliver the most value to? Who can you show up as your best self and do your best work for? Who can you make the biggest difference to?

Exercise 2: The PVP index

In *The 1-Page Marketing Plan*,[9] Allan Dib explains the PVP index, a concept he 'shamelessly stole from Frank Kern'.

PVP stands for personal fulfilment, value to the marketplace and profitability. The exercise involves rating each out of ten for any target market you are considering focusing on.

Personal fulfilment is how much you enjoy doing this particular work for a specific audience. Out of ten, how personally fulfilling would you find the work?

Value to the marketplace is how much your target market values your work and how much they're willing to pay for it. Out of ten, how highly would your target market value what you do?

---

9   A Dib, *The 1-Page Marketing Plan: Get new customers, make more money, and stand out from the crowd* (Successwise, 2016)

Profitability is how profitable the work is. Selling a high-priced product or service is not the same as having high profitability; the numbers need to work. Out of ten, how profitable would serving this particular audience be for you?

Obviously, the higher your overall score out of thirty, the more likely you are to have found your people and your business will be a success.

Exercise 3: Write their story

Once you've got the clarity you need on the work you want to do with the people you want to do it with, a powerful exercise is to write the story of your people. Write it out, like you would your own story. Talk about who they are, what they want and what's stopping them from having that.

This is not necessarily to share; this is just to help you get as much clarity as possible at this stage. I'll talk more about how to craft the stories you will be sharing in Chapter 9.

Writing out your people's story can be incredibly helpful.

For examples of stories I've written for clients, and a workbook to help you explore your people, go to www.thebusinessofstories.com/magic.

Make sure you capture the thoughts and ideas that have come up as you've worked through this chapter and any of the online exercises you've completed before you move on to exploring your value.

You're doing a great job! Keep up the good work.

 Storytelling magic

- Unpacking and exploring your stories can help you focus on a niche and an ideal client. In other words, it can help you find your people.

- The more specific you are about the people you want to work with, the more your message will speak to them.

- There is power in being specific about who you work with. You'll have a deep understanding of your target market and be able to share stories that truly resonate with them.

- Finding and serving your people will make you easier to remember and talk about. It will also make it easier for customers to say yes to working with you.

- To be truly happy and fulfilled in your work, make sure it rates highly on personal fulfilment, value to the marketplace and profitability.

7

Your Value

Coffee and connection

She wasn't having a great day before she'd even left the house.

She got in her ice-cold car and, after waiting for the freezing windscreen to thaw, she drove to the train station. She wasn't looking forward to the busy commute and she certainly wasn't looking forward to the meeting she had that morning.

As she approached the station, she was met with a wide, familiar smile. Heather Barrie of Harrie's Coffee had seen her drive in and already had her coffee on the go, just how she liked it, and her favourite bread browning in the toaster.

As the lady got closer, Heather sensed that she needed something else today. Before handing over her coffee, she gave her a warm, reassuring hug. She was right. It was just what the lady needed, and she really appreciated it. She even started to feel more positive about her day.

Does Heather sell coffee and toast or a familiar warm smile, a friendly face and a moment of connection in her customers' hectic, stressful lives? Your value goes way beyond the product or service you sell.

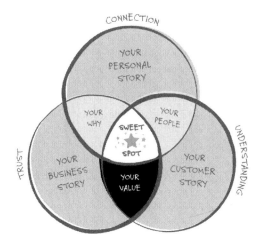

True value

Between your business story and your customer story is your *value*. It's the intersection between why your business exists and what you provide to the people you want to work with.

Your business is worthless if people don't see the value, to them, of what you do. They need to understand how you'll make their life better before they'll buy.

Let's explore that.

Are you helping the stressed-out CEO lose 20 lbs or are you helping them avoid burnout, or even a heart attack? Are you helping the young couple find a house or helping them find the home they will raise their family and create many lasting memories in? Are you helping the business owner work out what strategies they should focus on or build a business doing what they're brilliant at, so they can do more of the work they love with the people they love working with?

Sharing stories is a powerful way to demonstrate the true value of what you help people do. The more compelling your stories of success, the more people will understand what it is you're ultimately helping them achieve and the more valuable they will perceive your product or service to be.

That value might be the time or money you're saving them – mistakes can be costly – or the momentum you're helping them gather when they would otherwise have stood still. What is the true value of what you do for your client?

Separating yourself

In his book *Oversubscribed*,[10] Daniel Priestley talks about separating yourself from the market so you no longer have to compete with others. He says: 'If you're linking your business to the industry, to the market and to the trends that everyone else is following, then you'll continue competing on price with everyone else.'

---

10   D Priestley, *Oversubscribed: How to get people lining up to do business with you* (Capstone, 2020)

Exploring and understanding the value of what you do is a powerful way to stand out from the crowd and carve your own market. When people see and understand your true value to them and how you're going to make their life better, you will become more valuable in their eyes and can move away from being a commodity.

Why is that important? Being a commodity and offering the same as everyone else means you're inevitably going to have to compete on price, and that's a race to the bottom. As marketing guru Seth Godin says, 'The problem with the race to the bottom is that you might win'.[11]

Stories separate you from the rest of the market, showing (rather than telling) your true value and, in doing so, differentiating you from your competitors in a way they can never copy. When you do that, you're in a market of just one: you.

Go have fun

The people at Kingsland Wealth Management knew their value. Their ideal client is someone who wants to delegate all financial planning to an expert they trust, who will ensure their money is working

---

11   S Godin, 'The race to the bottom', *Seth's Blog* (20 August 2012), https://seths.blog/2012/08/the-race-to-the-bottom

hard for them so they can look to the future with confidence.

We worked together to switch their messaging from what they do:

'We are independent values-based financial planners, delivering fully comprehensive lifetime financial planning.'

...to the value they provide to their clients:

'We pore over the spreadsheets so you can go do the fun stuff.'

Then we crafted a story focused on how they give their clients freedom and security. We talked about the peace of mind that comes with clients knowing their money is being taken care of and someone is keeping them firmly on track to reach their financial goals.

While other financial planners talk about financial plans, the people at Kingsland talk about what is most important to their customers: living the life of their dreams while their money works hard for them.

Your process

Even if you don't think what you do is unique, you have a unique way of doing it. No one else does it exactly the same way. At the time of writing this book, I'm a StoryBrand Certified Guide and so are 773 other people, but we're all different. We all have our own style, way of working, experience, skillset and processes.

Your process will be different to anyone else's. Over the years, you will have found the things that work and what needs to be in place for you to help your customers get a great result. You'll have your way of explaining things, questions that you always ask and your own 'methodology' for helping your customer get to where they want to be. I have my Circles of Storytelling Magic. The process or method you have for getting a great result is part of the value you offer. It's part of your story.

Telling that story helps people see the value of what you do, that you know what you're doing, you've done it before, you have a tried-and-tested method and a formula or process that works. It's another layer of reassurance that you are the right person to help them.

Fifteen-minute call

Many years ago, I suffered from chronic fatigue. I was completely burnt out. It was a miserable time in my life. Every minute of every day was a struggle, and some days even lifting my arms felt so hard it was more than I could manage. For someone who approaches everything with a positive can-do attitude, it was pure torture. I cried. A lot.

Over the years, I tried everything. I spent thousands of pounds seeing doctors, therapists and specialists, trying every treatment, remedy and diet that was recommended. None of it helped and, in my lowest moments, I wondered if this was how the rest of my life was going to be.

Then someone mentioned a three-day course called The Lightning Process.[12] Always willing to try anything, I jumped on Google, found my nearest practitioner and picked up the phone.

I was probably on that call no more than fifteen minutes, but I came off totally believing that I had just found the answer to my prayers. I felt sure this was going to help me, despite the fact that nothing else had. I cried with relief.

When I think back to that short conversation, I know exactly why I felt so confident about it – because the practitioner I spoke to was so confident it would help me.

As we talked, she told me, 'You can do this!' and I believed her. I can't describe the immense relief and joy I felt in that moment. She knew the value she delivered, she knew how it would change my life and she made sure I knew it too.

I carried that confidence through the whole training and beyond. In fact, when it comes to my health, I carry it with me to this day.

---

12 P Parker, 'The Lightning Process', https://lightningprocess.com

I need to make something clear here: I'm not talking about making claims you can't deliver. I'm not endorsing the sort of 'hooks' you see on social media, promising to help you make £100K in the next thirty days with no product, no mailing list and no experience. That is *not* what I'm talking about at all.

I'm talking about standing in your value. I'm talking about confidently communicating what challenge you can help your clients overcome and who you can help them become. I'm talking about recognising, celebrating and sharing the value you deliver, the difference you make.

When you're confident about what you do and the results you help others get, your customers will feel it. They'll lean into it. They'll feel relieved, reassured and in safe hands. They'll be so glad they found you.

Don't compete

I was on a question-and-answer panel at a Women in Business event in Brighton. We had some interesting questions put to us and one in particular got me talking passionately about storytelling.

It was a question I'd heard many times before: 'How do I compete with a bigger brand?' The question came from a lady who had recently re-trained as an antenatal teacher and her worry was that she was competing against the National Childbirth Trust (NCT) that has over 114,000 members and a far bigger marketing budget than hers.

My answer was simple: don't. Don't try to be the NCT; be you. Tell stories that show how you are different. People who connect and resonate with your story will come to you.

You don't have to compete with anyone, just focus on doing what you do the way only you do it. This reminds me of a friend who, when he was a boxer, was constantly told by his trainer, 'Stop focusing on your opponent's game and what he's doing; focus on your game and what you're doing.'

Trying to compete with big brands – or anyone else, for that matter – is exhausting and demoralising. Instead, focus on your why, your people and your value. Share the stories that show your target market who you are, why you do what you do and, most importantly, what you can help them do. Focus on the value you deliver and your people will find you.

Being present

In August 2019, I had no intention of joining another coaching programme. I love a good mastermind and know the power of coaching, but I had decided to have a break from them for a while.

Then I got an email from someone I followed in my industry and an invitation to watch a video about his new coaching programme. At first, I resisted, but his email was good and the copy on his Facebook ads that magically started appearing in my feed grabbed my attention.

His messaging spoke to a feeling I knew very well, and when I read the email and watched the video, something he said hit me hard. He was talking about how, as a copywriter, he used to feel guilty whenever he was with his kids because, no matter how hard he tried, he just couldn't be fully 'present'. He'd try to switch his noisy mind off and not think about work for a few hours, but his head was always somewhere else. Often, he was feeling anxious about the project he was working on for a client, worried that they were not going to be happy with his work.

That short story triggered two feelings I was experiencing on an almost daily basis: guilt and anxiety. Guilt that I didn't spend enough time with my two girls. That I was not being a good mum when I needed to hide myself away in my office to work and take calls while they were at home. Anxiety that maybe my next client wouldn't be happy with my work, that it wouldn't be good enough. Both feelings were taking up a lot of space in my head and, when he called them out, it stopped me in my tracks.

He knew it. He'd been there. He got it and that meant he'd get me. He'd understand where I was at. He'd know what was holding me back and what I needed to do to be more of the person I wanted to be, at work and at home. He knew that between my story and his, there was a ton of value, and I immediately saw it too.

I trusted that he could help me deal with that guilt and anxiety because he'd successfully dealt with it himself. What did I do? I signed up for his programme: something I would not have done had he not told that story.

Exploring your value

Exercise 1: Be confident

For others to see your value, you need to see it first.

Too many business owners hesitate to tell people how they can help them. Their language is passive. They hang back, reluctant to make their offer, fearful of coming across as pushy or salesy.

I totally get that none of us wants to come across in that way, but there's a huge difference between being salesy and being confident that what you offer is incredibly valuable to the person who has the specific problem you can solve. If you're not super confident about what you do, you'll struggle to communicate your value to your clients.

Be confident in your offer. What are you confident about when it comes to your offer? What do you know you can help your clients do, be or have? What stories do you have about the difference your offer has made to your customers?

Be confident in your process. What are you confident about when it comes to your process? What result is your process designed to give your customers? What stories do you have about how your unique process has helped people solve the challenges they were facing?

Be confident in the results you help your clients get. What are you confident about when it comes to the results you help your clients get? What are some examples of happy ever after stories your clients have enjoyed? What has that enabled them to do?

Be confident in your pricing. What are you confident about when it comes to your pricing? Is it based on the value you deliver? Do you have any stories of how clients were able to quickly recoup their investment?

Be confident in how you help others achieve what they want to achieve. What are you confident about when it comes to the role you play in helping your customer win the day? At StoryBrand, we have a mantra: 'Be the guide'. What stories do you have of taking clients by the hand and leading them to success?

Exercise 2: What value?

You started your business to solve a problem. There are people who have that problem. Therefore, you have something of immense value to share.

If you can help your people get results that they have no idea how to achieve without your help, don't keep that a secret. Tell that story. If you want people to see your value, confidently stand in it.

Why is what you do so valuable to your customer? How is it improving their life and the life of those they serve? What is the true value?

Write down what you do, and then re-write it focused on the value it provides. For example:

What you do: we help you write your will.

Your value: we help you protect your family, your money and the assets you've worked so hard to build, and ensure your wishes really do come true.

 Go to www.thebusinessofstories.com/magic for more exercises and a workbook to help you explore your value.

Make sure you capture the thoughts and ideas that have come up as you've worked through this chapter and any of the online exercises you've completed, ready for us to look at them together in Part Three – Share.

Congratulations on all your hard work so far. We're going to be looking at the sweet spot in your Circles of Storytelling Magic next.

 **Storytelling magic**

- Sharing stories is a powerful way to demonstrate the true value of what you help people do.

- Exploring and understanding the value of what you do ensures you stand out from the crowd and carve your own market.

- Stories help you move from being a commodity and competing on price to being in a market of one: you.

- The process or method you have for getting a great result is part of the value you offer. It's part of your story.

- You don't have to compete with anyone. Just focus on doing what you do the way only you do it.

- Stand in your value. Be the guide and be confident in what you offer and the value you provide.

PART THREE: SHARE
Sharing the stories that speak to your people

8

The Sweet Spot

Dr Anna

Dr Anna had a lot of stories to unpack and explore, and she wasn't sure how they all connected or even if they did. Her work as a clinical psychologist and coach was varied and her clients different. She liked it that way. Her challenge was how to communicate what she does to different audiences with different needs and stories.

As we unpacked her personal, business and customer stories and joined the dots, we found the golden thread that ran through them. Her clients were different, but they were all 'performers' of one kind or another. Barristers working on high-profile cases; CEOs responsible for large organisations; actors with leading roles in London's West End shows: they were all driven, ambitious high-fliers who were performing at the top of their game — whether in a boardroom, a courtroom or on stage.

As a trained actress and regular guest on live TV shows, Dr Anna understood the challenges well. She knew the stakes were high. The pressure was on. The stress was intense. Anxiety could stop her clients from performing at their best. They were all susceptible to stage fright, breakdown or burnout.

With her fascinating, quirky blend of mindset coaching, fervent cheerleading and tough-love ass-kicking, she knew where she could make the biggest difference. She knew her why, she knew her value, she knew her people. We'd found the storyline that connected them all. We'd found her sweet spot, and we knew what stories to tell.

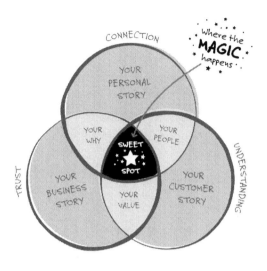

Whose story?

Before I jump in to talk to you about the exciting sweet spot right in the middle of your Circles of Storytelling Magic, let's just take a moment to reflect on all the work you've done so far. Please stop and think about what has come up for you during this process and how you're feeling about it. Maybe you have a deeper understanding of what you do and why, or a new level of clarity about who you want to do it for. Maybe you've had 'aha' moments and made connections that you've never made before. Maybe it's helped you cut away the clutter and get to the heart of what matters to you.

Whatever this journey so far has been for you, I want to thank you for playing all in, doing the work and trusting my process. Most business owners will never take the time to unpack and explore their stories the way you have, yet the impact of connecting and aligning your stories with the work you do and the people you do it for can be a complete game changer.

We're not finished, but you've done the heavy lifting and that deserves a little toast. To you and your stories. Cheers!

Intersecting stories

Now that you have some notes, reflections and thoughts about your personal, business and customer story, and you've explored them to find your why, the people you want to serve and the value you provide, let's talk about the magic sweet spot.

Your sweet spot is where all your stories come together and feel aligned and connected. It's where you truly understand who you are talking to; where you instinctively know what stories are going to resonate with your people to create connection, build trust and show that you recognise who they are, where they are and where they want to go.

Let's explore that some more.

It's from your sweet spot that you'll see where your story fits into your customer's story. Why is that important? Because if you're busy telling your own story with little regard for what's going on for your customer and how your story fits into theirs, you won't create a connection. At the same time, if you're only telling your customer's story without giving them a chance to understand who *you* are, they won't have a reason to choose you over someone else.

When business owners are confused about which parts of their story they should tell, it's usually because they don't have a deep enough understanding of their customer's story. The more you know about your people and their story, the easier it will be to know instinctively what stories will resonate with them.

 When you reach the sweet spot of your Circles of Storytelling Magic, you can tell the right story to the right person at the right time in their journey.

That, dear reader, is when the magic happens.

Goosebumps

Finding your sweet spot is not an exact science. It's intuitive. It's a feeling. When I'm talking to clients and I get goosebumps, I know we're getting to it.

When all of the stories you've unpacked and explored feel aligned and connected, you're probably there. When you understand your customer's story so well that you can stand in their shoes and feel what they're feeling, you'll know which parts of your personal story they're going to resonate with. When you understand what they're looking for, what they're worried about, where they're stuck and what help they need, you'll know how to talk to them about what you do, how you do it and what happy ever after you can help them achieve. When you're telling stories that create connection, build trust and inspire your people to take the first step on the quest they need to go on to make their life better, you'll know you've found the sweet spot. It's there, it's real and it's very powerful.

Coaching a racket

Ash Taylor enjoyed a successful career as a professional tennis coach for many years. He coached great players and grew his business to a significant size, with over thirty staff working across twelve venues and eighty schools. But in 2014, he switched from coaching tennis players to coaching business owners.

We worked together in the summer of 2021, when he wanted to create a message that would attract the right clients and help his business stand out in a crowded marketplace. He'd sent me a list of all the things he felt made him different, including creating a safe space, working on mindset and self-development, helping to give business owners direction and walking the walk, but as we chatted on our first call, something jumped out of his story.

He said, 'In all the years I was a tennis coach, I never once coached a tennis racket. I only ever coached the player to be the best player they can be.

'Business is the same. Anyone can teach the tactics and strategies, but that's like focusing on the racket first. It doesn't work that way round. You need to work out what kind of "player" you are first, what your unique style and natural swing is, and what type of "game" you want to play. The racket needs to fit the player just like the strategies need to fit the business owner, not the other way round. That's how you make sure you win.'

There it was. No amount of talking about mindset or direction was ever going to differentiate him like that little story. As well as getting to the essence of what he was about, it also spoke to the people he wanted to work with and to the value he delivered. His people were business owners who'd had enough of jumping from one marketing strategy to the next. They wanted help working out what kind of business owner they wanted to be and what they wanted their business to look like.

His words had perfectly aligned his personal story, business story and customer story. We'd found his sweet spot.

It's a jungle out there

Imagine this scene. You're standing at the edge of a jungle. On the other side of that jungle is something you really want. It's the life you want. The house you dream of building. The job you long to have. The love of your life. The health you want. The business you want. Whatever it is, it's there on the other side of the jungle in front of you.

As long as you can get through the jungle safely, you can have it, but there's a problem: getting through the jungle. You don't know the terrain. You don't know the way through. You don't know if there's a clear path or if you're going to get lost and never find your way out. You don't know what challenges you're going to face; whether you'll get attacked or eaten. You have no idea if you're going to make it to the other side in one piece. It's completely unknown territory.

It's a scary proposition and you feel ill-equipped and full of self-doubt, wondering if you even have what it takes to make it out the other side. You're stuck, rooted to the ground, too nervous to move.

Imagine, as you're standing there, feeling lost and unsure you'll ever get to where you want to be, someone appears at your side. They're dressed for the jungle, complete with boots, gaiters and leech socks, and they clearly know the territory. They've got a backpack, compass, bottles of water, various bits of equipment and a map, and look totally at home, like they've been here many times.

They speak to you. 'Hey, don't look so worried. I know this jungle like the back of my hand and it's not as scary as it looks. I've been through it many times. I know the quickest, safest route to take to get you through it and out the other side in one piece. I know how to avoid danger and make sure you don't get eaten.

'Let me take you by the hand and guide you safely through this jungle so you can have that thing you so badly want. We can do this, together.'

How are you going to feel? Relieved, right? When the right 'guide' turns up in your life, you're more than likely going to feel hugely grateful, hopeful, optimistic and happy. Maybe even excited to get started. The exact help you need has shown up at the exact time you need it.

That's how you want your customers to feel when they hear your story: relieved and grateful that you have appeared in their story just at the time they need you. Telling your story is about positioning yourself as the 'guide' that your customer needs.

In his book *Building a StoryBrand*,[13] Donald Miller talks about the importance of playing the role of the guide in your customer's story. He says that every human being is on their own 'journey of transformation' and

13 D Miller, *Building a StoryBrand: Clarify your message so customers will listen* (HarperCollins Leadership, 2017)

that we're all looking for our own guides to help us get to where we want to get to, achieve what we want to achieve and be the person we want to be. We all seek out those who can help us overcome the challenge we're facing, so that we can experience the transformation we want and become the person we want to be on the other side of that challenge. We want to find people who can truly help us win the day.

Your job is to position yourself and your brand as the guide for your customer.

Storytelling vs selling

What do you think when you hear the words 'sales funnel' or even 'selling'? Icky? When I asked that question in my Facebook group, the replies I got included 'Ugh!', 'Manipulative', 'Irritating', 'Forced' and 'Sleazy'. All negative and absolutely not how any business owner wants to feel, or make their customers feel.

But let's get real. If you're a business owner, you have to sell something. Otherwise, you don't have a business. You can't avoid selling, but you can do it in a way that it never feels 'salesy'.

That's one of the most powerful things about storytelling. If you do it right, you can have customers feeling delighted and grateful to buy from you without ever feeling salesy.

Think about my jungle story. We talked about feeling relieved, hopeful and excited to get going. No one I have told that story to has ever said, 'I'd feel sold to.' Why? Because our jungle guide makes us feel safe. In expert hands. Understood. Cared about.

That's the beauty of finding the sweet spot. The more you talk about how you can help your people navigate the journey ahead, with all its twists and turns, pits and potholes, and lead them safely out the other side to their final destination, the less they will feel sold to and the more relieved they will feel that you have appeared in their story.

Defining your sweet spot

Exercise 1: Stand in your sweet spot

Yay! You've arrived. Welcome to the sweet spot of your Circles of Storytelling Magic. This is where the magic happens.

I'm so excited for you. You've been on an incredible journey of discovery to get here and now you can start to reap the rewards of all the hard work you've done, but first, you need to put into words what your sweet spot looks, sounds and feels like.

To do this, go back through all your notes and stories and look for the golden thread. Think about what it is in those stories that connects you and your people. How are you like them? What parts of your stories feel in sync? Connected? What is it about your people that you 'get' on a deep level? Which parts of their stories can you truly relate to? What are the shared interests, values and beliefs?

If you have more than one audience, like Dr Anna at the start of this chapter, how are your different audiences the same? What is the theme that appears in all their stories? Take some time to think about what that sweet spot is for you and your people. Feel it. Tune into it. Describe it.

Then go to the sweet spot section of your workbook and write some statements about it.

Exercise 2: Define your sweet spot

As much as I want to put a formula together for you to help you find your sweet spot, I also want you to get that it is an intuitive thing. You need to go with what 'feels' right and a good fit, but I appreciate that's not always easy to do and might feel a little like you're inside the bottle, trying to read the label.

Here are some questions that might help you define it and craft a sweet spot statement so you can find the stories that are highly relevant and compelling for your audience.

What is common* about your customers' stories?
What stories can you share about that?

How are you like your clients? What stories can you
share about that?

**What is the golden thread* that links your personal,
business and customer stories together?** What stories
can you share about that?

What is the theme* of your combined stories? What
stories can you share about that?

**What expertise do you bring that makes you the
perfect guide?** What stories can you share about that?

How do you help your clients win the day? What
stories can you share about that?

*Golden thread, common and theme are all slightly
different. For Dr Anna, for instance, what was common
was that all her clients were 'performers' of one kind
or another. That's what linked them together and to
her story. The golden thread was that they all wanted
to perform at their best, but anxiety was getting in the
way of them doing that. The theme for all the stories
she would therefore be telling was that for them to
play full out and perform at their best, their head
needed to be in the right place.

Exercise 3: Your sweet spot statement

Use this formula to put your sweet spot statement
together. Remember this is just to help you define
your sweet spot so that you can go back through all

your notes from the exercises in Parts One and Two and find the stories that will be highly relevant and compelling for your people.

My clients are...

As a...

Together we...

So that...

Let's take Dr Anna as an example:

My clients are all performers of one kind or another, whether on stage, in a sporting arena or in a courtroom.

As a clinical psychologist, trained actress and TV presenter, I have a unique perspective when it comes to working with people who are under immense pressure to perform at their best.

Together we find the right tools and strategies that empower them to overcome their challenges, handle stress and manage their emotions.

So that they get to be the performer they were born to be.

 For more examples go to www.thebusinessofstories. com/magic.

Do not skip this step. It is where everything really comes together. This is where all your hard work pays off and you gain a much deeper understanding of the stories that will connect you and your people.

It's from your sweet spot that you'll intuitively know what stories are going to resonate with those that you want to attract into your world. You'll be ready to start crafting your stories and sharing them with the people you want to show up, ready to buy from you.

Huge congratulations! Amazing work. You've now tuned into your sweet spot and the magic of storytelling can begin.

 ## Storytelling magic

- Your sweet spot is where all your stories come together and feel aligned and connected.

- When you create connection, show understanding and build trust, you cut through the noise. You get heard and stand out.

- Telling your story is about positioning yourself as the guide that your customer needs, so that they feel safe, relieved and grateful.

- When you know the sweet spot of your Circles of Storytelling Magic, you can tell the right story to the right person at the right time in their journey. That is when the magic happens.

9
Crafting Your Stories

Flip-flops with a story

Rob and Paul Forkan, their two younger siblings and their parents had been travelling around the world for four years. Then the tsunami hit Sri Lanka on Boxing Day 2004 and their parents were tragically killed. The Sri Lankan people helped the children get home.

In 2012, Rob and Paul decided they wanted to build a children's home in Sri Lanka in their parents' memory. To fund this, they started a flip-flop business in their bedroom in Brixton with nothing more than a Facebook page. It was the start of what is now a global company called Gandys and everything about this inspirational brand is wrapped in their story.

The 'A' in the company name has a wave and represents overcoming adversity. The Kingfisher in their logo symbolises their dad's favourite beer. Their shirts have maps in the lining (they have since expanded to clothing and accessories with a travel theme) and the words 'Two brothers building homes for fellow orphans' are written on their flip-flops.

Their values are in their brand: 'Designed in London, inspired by travel, fuelled by giving back'. They've crafted a powerful story that continues to empower others and make a difference.

If a pair of flip-flops can tell a story of strength, commitment, fun, travel, helping others and being bold, what is possible for your brand?

Story loops

As you've got this far, you'll have at the very least thought about a few stories in your Circles of Storytelling Magic and have ideas about which ones will resonate with your people. Now let's look at things to keep in mind as you craft the stories you want to tell.

How you start and finish your stories is worthy of careful consideration. You're looking for a beginning that grabs people's attention. It doesn't have to be dramatic, but stories that hook people in pose a question that is compelling enough to keep them engaged.

They want to see how it's going to play out and how that question gets answered.

Our brain is programmed to resolve problems, so when a story opens a loop, it's hard not to keep watching, reading or listening until that loop is closed and the story resolved. Did the protagonist get what they wanted? Did they have what it took? Did they get past the thing that was holding them back? Did they make it all the way?

The main story question in *The Wizard of Oz* is whether Dorothy will ever get back home to Kansas. There are lots of mini story loops throughout to keep the viewer engaged. Will the scarecrow get his brain? Will the tin man get his heart? Will the lion get his courage? Will they ever make it to the Emerald City? Will they kill the bad witch? I'm sure you get the idea.

The end of your story is also super important and will determine how you leave people feeling and what they will remember. How do you feel at the end of *The Wizard of Oz* when Dorothy finally goes home? Happy that she's back with her family? Intrigued when you realise the people closest to her were the 'characters' walking alongside her all the time? Inspired that she already had everything she needed to get what she wanted – she just didn't realise it?

Think about the story loop you want to open, how you want your audience to be left feeling and what you want them to remember.

The chase

One of the biggest mistakes I see in storytelling is people putting way too much information into their stories. They include a ton of detail, like all the background information they think is relevant. I get it. It's hard to know what matters and what doesn't.

Many of us have had it drummed into us that every story has to have a beginning, middle and end, but think of your favourite action film. Where does it start? Right bang in the middle of the action, right? The hero in a high-speed car chase or running through a crowded market – usually being shot at. No filling in the background first. No explaining what the story is about. They just cut to the chase. Literally.

My point is this: your audience probably doesn't need to know everything that led up to the bit of your story they're going to connect with. You can just cut straight to the 'scene' that encapsulates what your story is about.

If you don't know how to do that, write out a story you want to tell, then delete the first two-thirds or anything that comes before the moment that sums up what your story is about. You'll be surprised how little of that background information you actually need to include for the story to work.

The four Cs

When it comes to crafting the stories you're going to tell, there are four Cs you need to pay particular attention to. They are the difference between a good story and a great story.

Remember, the best stories are easy to re-tell. Storytelling really gets magical and powerful when others are telling your stories for you.

For that to happen, they need to be clear, concise, compelling and congruent.

- **Clear:** Don't confuse your audience. Make sure the story is simple and easy to follow, and don't overshare. Any story you tell should come from the sweet spot of your Circles of Storytelling Magic so it's highly relevant and no one is confused about why you are sharing it. To keep people fully engaged, your story needs to flow, make complete sense and be simple to follow.

- **Concise:** Cut away the clutter. Stick to the stuff that matters and only include the details that need to be there and add value. Better to be specific and vivid about one particular moment than broad and vague about several. Every word must serve a purpose. People's attention spans are short, so respect their time by editing carefully and keeping your stories concise.

- **Compelling:** Your stories need to be compelling to keep people engaged. People love stories they can get lost in. It's why we watch movies, get hooked on shows on Netflix or look for books we can't put down. To engage your audience, the story needs to connect with them emotionally and take them on a journey. Look for places in your story where you can add intrigue, suspense, curiosity, vulnerability, honesty, humour or something unanticipated.

- **Congruent:** Congruency is key. When people engage with your stories, they'll want to feel like they're getting to know you, so if they engage with you or your business, they'll know what to expect. For that, your stories need to be consistent and congruent through every interaction with every customer, every time. The stories you're telling need to be true to the experience your customers are having. The more real, honest and true you are, the easier it will be to stay congruent.

La la land

Any story you tell should be relevant. Know why you're telling it, but at the same time, resist the temptation to spell it out for your audience. Let them decide what your story means to them. Let them reflect on how your experiences and lessons relate to theirs.

When I watched the film *La La Land*, I loved it and spent ages afterwards thinking what the moral of the story was. I asked my husband what he thought. He said that the guy should have been more flexible and followed the girl, and they could both have fulfilled their dreams. My daughter took that sometimes a couple can do more for each other by taking separate roads than they can by staying together. My hairdresser (who better to discuss these things with?) took that sometimes you have to let go of the people you love to let them follow their passion.

Who's right? There is no right or wrong, just our own interpretation.

What matters is that your audience takes something positive from your story and feels a little more connected to you for hearing it.

Write with personality

I'm not a huge fan of 'rules' when it comes to storytelling, or when writing any copy or content for that matter. I prefer to focus on what sounds good. What flows well. What will connect and resonate with the audience.

Conversational-style writing is intimate, personal and engaging, so rather than getting fixated on the rules, I encourage my clients to write with personality. Here are my top three tips on how to do that.

1. Use everyday words

Focus less on being 'professional' and more on being personal. Keep your language simple. I know it's tempting to use words and phrases that demonstrate your level of knowledge and expertise, but clear and simple beats clever and complicated every day.

I write in a way that my eleven-year-old daughter can read, understand and engage with. I kept her in mind as I wrote this book, hoping she will read it. Hi, Daisy!

Many people find that as soon as they sit down to write or type something that comes under the banner of 'marketing', a strange thing happens. Their writing becomes stiff, a little formal and a million miles away from what they sound like in real life. Suddenly, they don't know how to sound like themselves. Strange, right?

The easiest way I know to get over this is to speak the first draft of anything into your phone while you walk your dog. OK, the dog isn't mandatory, but walking outside definitely helps to get you in a more relaxed, free-flowing state of mind.

As you talk, don't worry about getting it right or editing. Just talk, naturally and conversationally. Don't think 'content' or 'marketing'; think 'chatting to a friend'.

When you get back home, you can use a transcription tool like otter.ai. Then you can edit. Take out the ramblings and repetitions to keep it concise and punchy, but don't change the tone or conversational style. You want it to sound like you.

2. Write for your people

Please don't write for everyone. You can't. It's impossible. If you don't believe me, go to Amazon, click on any book and read the reviews. Chances are, there'll be glowing five-star reviews and scathing one-star reviews. Same book. Different readers.

Now that you know the sweet spot in your own Circles of Storytelling Magic and you've dived into who your people are, write for those people. Write for the person who will like your stuff; appreciate your viewpoint; reply when you send emails out to your list; thank you for the tips, content and recommendations you post on social media; share your content and happily recommend you to others. The person who will resonate with your posts because they were having the exact same conversation in their own head just this morning. The person who feels inspired and motivated to step up and be who they want to be because of how your story touched them.

Be you and you'll attract the people that get you. Like you. Trust you. That person might not have come across you yet, but they're out there. Write for them.

3. Find your voice

Great writing is fearless. I'm not suggesting you rant, but don't be afraid to share your thoughts and ideas. Have an opinion. Start conversations. Get people thinking. Throw ideas out there. Share your unique perspective. Ask questions.

Talk to your audience as an equal. You don't need to know everything about your topic to start a discussion, share your thinking or create connections. You can be a contributor without labelling yourself a guru. As Denise Duffield-Thomas, author of *Get Rich, Lucky Bitch*, says, 'Who cares if you don't know everything. You don't have to be the best to make a difference to someone.'[14]

Your storytelling will be better if you focus on having meaningful conversations with people who will engage and resonate with you, rather than thinking you need to be 'the expert'. Writing is a joy when you

---

14 D Duffield-Thomas, *Get Rich, Lucky Bitch! Release your money blocks and live a first-class life* (CreateSpace, 2013)

forget the rules, stop worrying about getting it 'right', find your voice and just speak to the person who will welcome you into their mad, crazy, full-on life like a friend as they stop for a moment to engage with your stories. Talk to them.

Corporate speak

I've had clients tell me they worry that if they don't use the kind of jargon and corporate speak that's the norm in their industry, they'll lose credibility. That those coming to their website will be expecting it.

That's precisely the problem. Every other business owner is using the same language and they all sound the same.

How can you sound different if you're saying exactly what everyone else is? How can you stand out if you're using the same language your competitors use?

Corporate speak makes it hard to connect as a human. Taking the time to get your message and story across in a way that is refreshingly different and not reliant on overused and meaningless jargon shows that you're prepared to put the work in so your customer can have a better experience. You're not sending them into a mind-numbing trance with the boring words and tired phrases that are rife in your industry, or in marketing in general. Instead, you're engaging them with simple and compelling messages and stories.

 When you ditch the jargon and speak to your audience from the heart, standing out gets a whole lot easier.

Crafting your stories

Exercise 1: Cut to it

Go back to the defining moments you unpacked in Chapters 2 and 3. Tell a story about one of those, starting right in the moment. No need to fill in the background. Just start in that moment.

Here's an example.

When my daughter was nine years old, we were standing at the bottom of a huge flight of stairs in a cinema in Epsom, Surrey. We were holding hands. She was chatting excitedly about seeing the movie. I was silently crying. I didn't have the energy to walk up the stairs with her and I felt utterly overwhelmed with frustration and guilt. It was one of the lowest moments in my battle with chronic fatigue, but also an important turning point and the catalyst for an incredible journey that led to me becoming the guide and storyteller I am today.

Where could your story start? Choose a defining moment and start your story there.

Exercise 2: Five senses

Great stories engage more than one of our senses. In my short story in Exercise 1, I used:

Sight: 'huge flight of stairs in a cinema'

Touch: 'holding hands'

Sound: 'chatting excitedly', 'silently crying'

Feelings: 'overwhelm, frustration and guilt', 'one of the lowest moments in my battle with chronic fatigue'

Add more depth to any story by describing what you saw, heard, smelt, touched or tasted. You don't need to go into a ton of detail, just enough to move your audience from being here, listening to you, to being there in the story with you.

Exercise 3: Structure

It's important that your stories have structure. Structure helps ensure the story is clear, that it flows, makes sense and is in a logical order that people can easily follow. Structure helps you take your audience on a journey.

Somebody wanted but so then is a simple formula you can use to help make sure your stories have some structure. For example:

Somebody: who is the main character? Dorothy is the main character in *The Wizard of Oz*.

Wanted: what did the character want? She wanted to get back home to Kansas.

But: what was the problem? Her house had been destroyed. She didn't know where she was or how to get back home.

So: what did the character do to try and solve the problem? She followed the Yellow Brick Road to the Emerald City to ask the wizard if he could help her get back home.

Then: what was the resolution to the story? She clicked her heels together, said 'There's no place like home' and returned to her loved ones.

Once you have outlined your story based on the structure above, you can expand on it to create depth, intrigue and conflict (see Exercise 4). As you do so, stick to the structure to ensure your stories flow and make sense to your audience.

Exercise 4: Adding depth

There are many ways to add depth to your stories so they are more compelling. Try these:

Timeline. Giving a specific date or some indication of a timeline somehow makes a story more powerful and real. It helps give context and answer questions in your audience's mind about when things happened and in what order.

In Chapter 1, I started a story with:

It was 7pm on Thursday 26 May 2016 when I heard the comment that would completely change the trajectory of my business. How much more credible and powerful is that than if I'd simply said, 'One day a few years ago...'?

Conflict. Introducing conflict builds tension and keeps your audience gripped. A story doesn't really get interesting until we know what the conflict is.

Conflicts can be both external and internal. An ex-employee taking all your clients is an external conflict, while feeling hopeless and paralysed with self-doubt is an internal one. Introducing the conflict, and then telling how you overcame that challenge to get the resolution you wanted will give your story a compelling beginning and end.

Intrigue. Once you have introduced the conflict, it will be easier to add suspense and intrigue to your story as you leave questions hanging in the air - will Dorothy ever get back to Kansas? Talk about tough choices you had to make or moral dilemmas you were faced with. Use cliff hangers to keep people engaged and vary the pace, mood and tension levels so your story feels like a real journey, with all its inevitable ups and downs.

Positivity. Your audience won't appreciate stories that leave them in a negative state. Absolutely talk about the challenges and hard times faced by both you and your clients, but with a positive message that leaves the audience feeling good. This is about standing *on* your story, not *in* it. Notice how my story in Exercise 1 finished in a positive way and ensured I didn't leave you feeling bad for me.

Dialogue. Using dialogue in your story helps bring it to life. Be careful not to overdo it, though, with long pieces of dialogues or too many of them. Short snippets of conversation can really help your audience feel like they were there.

There are several stories in this book where I've used dialogue, including the comment in Chapter 1 from the business start-up manager: 'Hmmm, well, I was kinda hoping you'd be at the front of the room – delivering it.'

Stakes. When we engage in a story, whether we realise it or not, there's a question we want answered quickly. Why should we care?

For a story to keep us engaged, something has to be at stake. What happens if this situation doesn't change? What if I hadn't got my health back on track? What would life look like for me and my daughter? Your audience will want to know what's at stake; why it matters and why they should care. As you write your stories, keep the stakes in mind.

Sense. When your story is ready, do a sense-check by reading it out loud. I learned this when I started reading the copy I'd written out to clients. No matter how much I thought it all made sense in my head, it wasn't until I was reading it out loud that I noticed sentences that were repetitive or too long, or that something didn't quite work the way I thought it did in my head. Now I never share anything until I've read it out loud at least once to check it's clear, concise and as interesting as it can be.

Use the workbook at www.thebusinessofstories. com/magic to write a story using the above guidelines and concepts.

Huge congratulations. All your hard work is about to pay off, as you craft stories that will connect and resonate with your people.

 ## Storytelling magic

- Write with personality. Use everyday words. Write for your people and share your unique perspective.

- How you start and finish your stories is important and worthy of careful consideration. Define your story loops and what you want to leave your audience with.

- Cut to the chase. Your audience probably doesn't need all the background information you think you need to tell them.

- Let your audience decide what your story means to them. Resist the temptation to tell them what they should have taken away.

- Remember the four Cs. Make sure your stories are clear, concise, compelling and congruent.

10
Sharing Your Stories

Mum's care

In 2016, my sister and I were looking for an agency that could provide care in the home for our elderly mother. Naturally, we wanted to find one that we felt totally confident would provide a high standard of care and attention, but who to trust?

The search began and we both spent a lot of time on the internet, looking at what each agency offered in terms of where it was based, what kind of services it provided and what it charged. Gathering factual information that we could list and compare was fairly straightforward, but it didn't help us make a decision about who we wanted to use as it was difficult to see why we would choose any of them over the others.

Then I landed on a website that had a tab called 'Our Story'. I clicked on it. Of course I did.

The MD of this agency had been a TV presenter for Sky News when her husband had needed palliative care in their own home in what she described as her 'personal trauma tsunami' of February 2013. As a result of what she and her husband had gone through and the amazing care and support that helped them both through it, her appetite for her TV career evaporated forever.

Losing her husband left a void in her life that she wanted to fill in a meaningful way, and she dreamed of setting up a company that would provide the high quality of care that she felt everyone should expect and demand for their own loved ones. That company stood out from a long list of possibilities and gave my sister and me a story to connect with. In just a couple of short paragraphs, we knew the MD's why, her value and the one thing that was completely unique: her story. We knew she had first-hand experience of what we were currently going through, and we felt confident she would understand our concerns and why it was so important for us to find the right person to look after our mum.

That short story had given us a reason to choose her agency.

Every business has a story

It's important to remember that while every business owner has a story that is unique, *having* a story isn't. The owners of any of the agencies we looked at could have told us their story. They all have one.

Every company starts with someone wanting to make it happen, and then working hard to bring it to life. Someone with a vision. Someone who wants to make a difference. The founder or business owner might not be front and centre, the brand might not be about them, but every business is made up of people.

People brought each and every one of those agencies we looked at into existence. Each one of them cares for people's loved ones, and people have stories. The only thing this agency did differently from every other one we looked at was take the time to unpack, craft and share their story.

Story wins. Can you really afford not to be sharing yours?

Happy-ever-after stories

Whatever your business, sharing happy customer stories ticks a lot of boxes. They show potential customers what's possible and that getting the same result is possible for them too.

Success stories speak volumes. They show you know what you're doing, that your process, product or service works, and that other people have had a positive outcome as a result of engaging with you. They bring what you do to life.

Nothing says 'My stuff works' louder than stories of people who have experienced a transformation. People who are in a different place, further on in their journey than they were before they bought your product or service. People who solved the problem that was stopping them from having, doing or being what they want, thanks to your business offer. Whether they're now a calm parent, savvy investor, home decorating ninja, confident cook or engaging teacher, stories of how they overcame the challenges and went on to win the day, with your help, will be compelling to your people.

Whenever I'm talking to potential clients about the possibility of working together, I always tell lots of stories and walk them through 'before and after' examples of people, businesses and brands I've worked with. Personally, I need to 'see' what something looks like before I buy it. I want to understand what's going to be different, what I'm going to have afterwards that I don't have now and how that's going to make my life better. When I can see real-life examples of the difference other people have experienced, it makes it easier for me to commit to action and take the next step, and I'm not alone in this. Your people likely need the same.

Don't forget to craft and share your happy-ever-after stories.

Looking small

'Will telling my story make me look small?' asked a client. He was referring to the fact that he wanted to be seen as a brand rather than a one-man band.

Telling your story doesn't make you look small; it makes you look real. Richard Branson, Elon Musk, Tony Robbins and Sheryl Sandberg are great storytellers – they all give frank and honest accounts of their journey, their successes, their failures, their philosophy, their values, their goals and their vision. I don't think anyone could accuse them of looking small.

If you want to inspire and connect with others, as you share your vision and become seen as a thought leader, start with your story.

Where to share

Stories are compelling, magical and everywhere. We've unpacked and explored a lot of stories in your Circles of Storytelling Magic, but also look around you for more stories that can add value, intrigue and narrative to your products and services, and help bring them to life. Then share them. Regularly.

There are so many places and so many ways you can share your stories: videos, podcasts, interviews, articles, posts and in every conversation you have about what you do, online and in person. Here are just a few suggestions to get you started.

Social media

Social media is all about storytelling. It's what people expect, so it's a great place to try your stories out. Keep them simple and short. Share something about the people in your business to humanise your brand. Share something you've learned or a challenge you're facing right now. Talk about stuff that matters to your people and ask questions. Be a contributor.

Think about the questions you get asked all the time and share stories that help to answer them. Take note of what's happening around you as you run your business and share stories about it. Record what's going on for you and your customers and chop it up into bite-size stories you can share.

Not every story you put out will create a ton of engagement and that's OK. Focus on doing it consistently and sharing stories from your sweet spot, and you'll attract your target market.

Email campaigns

Emails are a powerful way to engage your audience with storytelling as you get to have a one-on-one conversation with someone who has already invited you into their inbox. Use stories to build a genuine connection and nurture the new relationship. Think about the jungle scene I talked about in Chapter 8. How can you be the guide for your people? What is their 'jungle' and how can you show that you know how to guide them through it?

Stories of what your clients have achieved are powerful, as are stories about what you do differently from other people or your unique perspective. Look back at the stories you've unpacked and explored as you've worked through this book. You'll have a ton that could be shared. No matter what you want to email your list about, look for ways to incorporate short stories into your message.

Remember to open a story loop, but you don't always have to close it in the same email. You could leave your audience wanting more with a cliffhanger that encourages them to read the next email.

Your website

There are many ways to incorporate storytelling into your website. Of course, there's your own story, which I highly recommend you share on your 'About' page.

I struggle with websites that don't have an 'About' page, or which have one that doesn't tell me anything about the person or people behind the brand.

People want to know who they are buying from. Think of the examples in this book, like the couple in the market in Salisbury or the TV presenter with a care agency. By sharing their stories, they enabled me to connect with *who* they are and what they're about, which made the buying decision a whole lot easier. People buy from real people.

Your website should also tell your customer's story. Use the *somebody wanted but so then* structure I outlined in the previous chapter to show that you understand what your customer wants, what's in the way of them having it and what success will look like when they've worked with you.

Sales conversations

I love chatting to business owners who want to get better at telling stories. It helps that I'm so curious and genuinely want to know about them and their business. I ask questions like, 'Why do you do what you do?' or simply, 'What's your story?' Keeping my questions open gives them free rein to tell me whatever they want to, which is usually what matters to them most. I'll also share a short story about me and what I love about what I do, and stories about my clients.

Of course, when you're chatting to prospects who are interested in working with you, you'll need to answer the 'How does it work?' and 'How much does it cost?' questions, but make sure you look for opportunities to naturally weave stories into the conversation too. Always keep the stories short and relevant. Use them to spark interest and curiosity, create connection and ensure you both leave the conversation feeling like you got to know each other a little more.

Testimonials

Getting testimonials from your clients will give you some of the best, most powerful stories you can share, but there are some things you need to do to make sure the testimonials you get tell a story that is compelling to others.

Here are the four questions I ask every client at the end of a project:

1. What was the problem you wanted to solve and how was having that problem making you feel?

2. How did you find the process and working with me and my team? What did you find most helpful?

3. What do you now have as a result of working with us? What difference has that made to you and your business?

4. What would you say to someone who is sitting on the fence about using my product/service?

The answers to these questions help me share stories that will be interesting to my people. For more tips on how to get great testimonials from clients, go to www.thebusinessofstories.com/magic.

Storytelling for products

It would be easy to think that storytelling only works for service-based businesses, but that's not true. Any type of business can harness the power and magic of storytelling. Gandys (see Chapter 9) is one of my favourite examples of a brand that weaves storytelling into everything it does. Here's another awesome example of a brand that uses storytelling to sell its products.

Storybook cosmetics

Identical triplets Erin, Mandy and Missy were bringing out a new range of cosmetics. They had not even launched yet, but due to overwhelming demand, they had to stop taking orders for their first product: a set of five make-up brushes.

They had only posted about thirty pictures on their new Instagram account, but had amassed over 100K followers in a few days. They were the number-one trending topic on Facebook within a couple of days of setting up their page. To say they were oversubscribed before launching was an understatement.

What was so special about their cosmetics? They were all based on stories. Their set of five make-up brushes were adaptations of the *Harry Potter* wizard wands, namely Harry's, Ron's, Dumbledore's, Hermione's and Lord Voldemort's.

Since then, they've introduced 'storybooks' of make-up based on classic novels such as *Little Women*, *Sherlock Holmes* and *Robin Hood*. They also have a *Hunger Games* range of highlighters, including Revolution, Beacon of Hope and Girl on Fire.

Their 'About' page starts 'Once upon a time there were three sisters who never stopped believing in fairy tales...' and they've attracted a lot of attention. Last time I checked, they'd been featured in *The Huffington Post*, *Cosmopolitan*, *Glamour* magazine, *The Today Programme* and *BuzzFeed*.

Their phenomenal success started with a love of storytelling.

I hope by now, you understand just how powerful storytelling is and why you need to be using it in your business. Storytelling isn't just a 'nice to have' or a one-off exercise; it's something you need to be doing constantly if you want to attract and engage more of the people you love working with.

A story grabs people's attention like nothing else can. It's a superpower and businesses that are harnessing it stand out. But, just in case you still think a nice-looking brochure will do fine, let me tell you what happened when I took my shiny, new hot-off-the-press brochure to a business accelerator programme in London in 2016.

I arrived early and put one on each of the forty or so seats that would be occupied by entrepreneurs. During the tea break and over lunch, several of my fellow attendees congratulated me on getting my brochure done and commented on how nice it looked – but no one enquired about working with me.

About an hour before the end of the day, the facilitator invited me to speak to the group about what I do. I jumped at the chance, even though I was so nervous I could barely breathe. I've had a fear of public speaking since I was at school, and I was shaking so much I nearly dropped the microphone.

Rather than ignore my obvious anxiety in that moment, I opened with a story about the strange thing that happens to me when someone puts a microphone in my hand. I talked about how I start shaking, sweating and practically hyperventilating, but I am so passionate about helping people tell their story, I'm prepared to put myself through this ordeal to reach the people I know I can help. I got real and vulnerable, and saw a sea of smiling faces and encouraging looks from the audience as they empathised and willed me on.

I was still shaking when I sat down, but when the workshop came to an end just under an hour later, several people came over to talk to me. By the time I left the hotel that day, I had six new clients.

Sharing your stories

Share your stories and people will relate to you. Share your stories and people will connect with you. Share your stories and people are more likely to be interested in the journey you can take them on with your business offering.

Exercise 1: Start with one

What's one short story you could share today from your personal or business journey that will resonate with your people? Use the tips and exercises in Chapter 9 to write and structure it. Then share it, either in person or online.

Exercise 2: Everyone wins

Think about a story that shows your expertise, your value and how you help your customers win the day. This book is full of short stories I've written about my clients that also demonstrate my expertise and show that my process works.

Exercise 3: Stories of transformation

Share a testimonial from a client that says, in just a couple of sentences, what was going on for them before they bought your product or service, and what's going on for them now. These short stories of transformation will be compelling to people who want to experience that same transformation. For more tips on how to get great testimonials from clients, go to www.thebusinessofstories.com/magic.

Use the workbook at www.thebusinessofstories. com/magic to plan the stories you want to share over the coming weeks and months. There is a content planning sheet to help you.

You did it. You've come so far. You have your stories to share with the people waiting to hear them. Great job!

Storytelling magic

- Every business has a story to tell. Businesses are made up of people and people have stories.

- Success stories speak volumes. Nothing says 'My stuff works' louder than the stories of people who have experienced a transformation as a result of working with you.

- Share the stories in your Circles of Storytelling Magic and look around you for everyday stories that can add value, create intrigue and bring your products and services to life.

- Share your stories everywhere: on social media, in your email campaigns, on your website and in your sales conversations.

- Storytelling is a superpower. Can you really afford not to be using it in your business?

11

The Most Important Story

Bread, Marmite and Pot Noodles

As I write this book, I've been reading Happy Sexy Millionaire by Steven Bartlett.[15] He tells the story that when he was twenty-five, the tech company he founded at twenty-one was listed on the stock exchange with a valuation of $200 million. In just four years, he'd become one of the richest under-thirties in the UK at that time. Yet he felt absolutely nothing. Nada. Numb. Empty.

Compare that to a day just a few years earlier when, aged eighteen, he found £13.40 in loose change down the back of some seats in a takeaway shop. At that time, he was unemployed, penniless and living in a

---

15 S Bartlett, *Happy Sexy Millionaire: Unexpected truths about fulfilment, love and success* (Yellow Kite, 2021)

rundown house in the most dangerous part of Manchester. He had gone to the takeaway shop to see if he could find some half-eaten chicken left on a table before it got cleared away. Finding £13.40 meant he could actually buy enough bread, Marmite and Pot Noodles to last a few days. He was sooo happy!

Why did £13.40 make him happy when $200 million didn't? I'll come back to that in a minute.

The story in your head

I couldn't write a book about storytelling without talking about something I'm absolutely passionate about. The story that makes all the difference. The most important story of all.

It's the one you're telling yourself – all day, every day.

This is something I've struggled with and had to work on my entire life. I know I'm not alone because I see, hear and feel it happening with the people I meet, work with and spend time with every day.

The problem is, if you're telling yourself a story that's negative, you're unlikely to feel good about sharing it with others. You're not going to want to put yourself out there and be honest, real and vulnerable if you're already giving yourself a hard time about not being good enough. We need to change that story so you can tell yourself a new one.

I've read a lot of mindset books over the years but, for me, one of the most helpful, practical and easy-to-implement is *Soundtracks* by Jon Acuff.[16] In his book, Jon talks about the negative 'soundtracks' we're constantly listening to in our heads: the conversations we have with ourselves as we wake, go through our day and go to bed. If your inner 'chats' are negative, they'll hold you back from ever taking action on all the things you want in life. Your thinking will totally get in the way of what you want.

Over the years, you'll have built a soundtrack for your career. Your business. Your relationships. Your hopes and every other aspect of your life. As Jon Acuff points out in his book, one of the greatest mistakes you can make in life is assuming your soundtracks are true. Most of the time, they're complete rubbish.

Being in charge of the soundtrack you're running in the background is critical and Jon suggests three simple actions you can take today to change the soundtrack from negative to positive:

- **Retire** your negative soundtracks.

- **Replace** them with new ones.

- **Repeat** them until they're as automatic as the old ones.

---

16   J Acuff, *Soundtracks: The surprising solution to overthinking* (Baker Books, 2021)

It really is as simple as that.

Here are three questions you can ask yourself about the soundtrack you have running in your head right now:

- Is it true?

- Is it helpful?

- Is it kind?

If you've answered no to any of those questions, you need a better soundtrack.

Steven Bartlett explains in his book how he changed his mindset from numb to happy by changing the conversation he was having with himself in his head. Instead of expecting happiness to show up because of the money he'd just made, he took time to reflect on how far he'd come and feel immense gratitude for everything that had happened along the way. The people he'd met. The journey he'd been on. The learning and growing he'd experienced. In doing so, he changed the way he felt and was able to appreciate where he was today and what he'd achieved. He was able to feel happy and proud.

As Steven points out, gratitude didn't happen automatically. He had to invite it in, and so will you. You have to practise it. You have to train your brain to think that way.

Choosing your story

When you stop consuming content that doesn't make you feel good and instead feed your mind with better, more life-enhancing content, you change your story. When you stop comparing yourself to others, and instead focus on the incredible and magical adventure you are having, you change your story. When you take time to notice all the things around you to be grateful for and get more intentional about what you think about and focus on, you change your story.

Don't let the good stuff – the wins, the moments to cherish and celebrate, the events and people to feel grateful for – slip by, unnoticed and unacknowledged. Be in charge of your story. Make it a good one.

Your story isn't already written. You are writing it as you live it, every moment of every day. The next scene doesn't have to go the same as the last one did or the one before that. It doesn't have to be the same as anyone else's or conform to what other people have decided is the norm.

Every morning when you wake up, you get to choose how your story goes, moment by moment. You can change it any time you want.

If you want to see how different and varied and fascinating people's stories are, take a look at Humans of New York.[17] Started as a photography project in 2010, it had an initial goal to photograph 10,000 New Yorkers to create a 'catalogue of the city's inhabitants'. These portraits, along with an accompanying quote or short story, became a blog providing daily glimpses into the lives of thousands of strangers on the streets of New York City. That blog now has over 20 million followers on social and has become the subject of two bestselling books.

No two stories are the same and no one gets to decide what is right or wrong for someone else. Your story is your story, and you are the author of it. Own it. Take charge of it. Write it. Live it.

Legacy

In 2020, my eldest daughter Amy hired a genealogist to research our family tree on my dad's side. She then created a beautiful scrapbook full of little stories, images, recorded entries and wonderful gems of information about our family history. It is fascinating to read, and we've all spent time together, going through it and learning so much about where we come from. She may have done it for my dad, but it was a wonderful gift for all of us and something that will be passed on to future generations and enjoyed by family members for many years to come.

---

17 Humans of New York: www.humansofnewyork.com

Part of choosing the story you want to live, and sharing it with others, is the legacy you want to leave behind. A little bit of you will live on in the stories that are told about you. Part of your legacy could be something you've done professionally. Simply by creating a business that has meaning and purpose, and doing the work you love with the people you love working with, you show others what is possible for them too. That is a legacy you'll never know the full ripple effect of. As I write this book, my hope is that these words will inspire people to share their story for years to come, even after I've left this world.

Your legacy is also about how you make people feel, what you inspire them to do, what values you share and what others learn from you. Being honest, open and vulnerable, sharing the ups and downs and telling stories that motivate others to keep going when life feels hard is a powerful legacy. We all leave an impression on this Earth; we all leave some kind of legacy. Being in charge of your story and deciding how you want to show up every day means you get to influence what impression you leave and how long it will live on.

Here are some things I try to do on a regular basis to help me stay in charge of my own story. I say 'try' because I am far from perfect at it, but I have noticed that it is the times when I don't feel like doing these things that I need to do them the most.

Capture, create and practise the soundtracks you want to hear. When I signed up to a book-writing programme and committed to getting this book planned, written and published in six months, the negative chitter chatter kicked in – with a vengeance. I immediately stuck a piece of paper on my wall and jotted down the soundtracks I wanted playing in my head every time I thought about working on my book. They included, 'A book is words and I *love* writing words'.

Notice things to be grateful for. At any given moment of any day, you can find something to be grateful for. I like journaling, but I'm not good at doing it every day, and if I start giving myself a hard time about not doing it, I just feel bad, which completely defeats the object. What I try to do instead, several times a day, is take a second to express gratitude for something. Delicious food. Lovely smells. A smile. A hug. The weather. My health. A good book. Writing that flows.

When you look for things to be grateful for, you'll find the list is endless.

Be your own mentor, coach and guide. This takes practice, but it's a game changer when you switch from critic to coach. For me, the first thing was to believe that I am good enough and catch myself every time I doubt my ability or worth. I try to be kind, compassionate and gentle with myself, and never say anything to myself that I wouldn't say to one of my gorgeous daughters.

Never compare yourself to others. This is hard, particularly when every time you check social media, you see what everyone else is doing, having and being. It can leave you feeling that your life isn't interesting enough, your achievements are not good enough or your goals are not big enough.

There are two things I always remind myself:

- Those are people's feeds, not their complete lives. Big difference.

- You can't compare yourself to anyone else because their life, circumstances, experiences, wants and challenges are different to yours.

You never know what's really going on for other people. By all means, follow people you admire and who make you feel good when you read, listen to or watch their stuff, but other than that, focus on what you're doing – your goals, your growth – not what anyone else is doing.

Stay in charge of your story. You are the author of your story. You decide how it plays out, where it goes and what it focuses on. Of course, things will happen that you didn't plan for; life throws curveballs, but you can stay firmly in the writing seat. You still get to choose how you deal with the twists and turns, how you show up and what you tell yourself about yourself from moment to moment.

Changing your story

Exercise 1: Hero or villain?

It's the story you're running in your own head that will have the biggest impact on how you show up in the world, what you will achieve and how you will feel about whatever the next month, year or decade brings. That's the story that will dictate what your happy ever after will be.

How does that story, the one you're running in your head, make you feel? And who writes *that* story? You.

I've found the more I take charge of my story, with the themes, plots, storylines, characters, transformations and endings I want to show up and experience, the truer that story becomes. Take some time to consider whether the story you're telling yourself is serving you or if it needs some reworking. Are you the hero of your own story or the villain? Are you standing up for what you believe in or knocking yourself down at every opportunity? Are you your biggest cheerleader or your biggest critic?

What story do you want to be living? How do you want it to play out? Where do you want it to go? How can you invite yourself into the story you want to be living?

Exercise 2: What will they say?

One of the most powerful exercises I've ever done is to consider what I want people to say about me after I'm gone. For me, it was an incredibly emotional and enlightening exercise, involving a lot of tears, smiles and 'aha' moments, and it's one that I regularly go back to and review.

How do you want to be remembered? What do you want your friends and family to say about you? What about your peers, colleagues and employees? What stories do you want people to recall and share? What is the legacy you want to leave?

Write it all down.

Here's the thing: people are only going to say those things if that's how you show up. Every moment of every day, you are living a life that people will remember, whether that's in a good light or bad. It's up to you to live a life that, after you've gone, people will remember the way you want them to.

You can reverse engineer it. Decide what you want your story and legacy to be, then go bring that story to life.

Exercise 3: Three words

Ask some people that know you to describe you in three words.

When I was asked recently by a personal brand photographer to describe myself in three words, I decided to see what others thought about me.

The responses I got back from friends, colleagues and clients made me feel incredibly proud and grateful.

The words they used included inspirational, funny, insightful, empathetic, loving, down to earth, determined, gregarious, vivacious, and effervescent.

Apart from making my day, this exercise did a few things. First, it helped me see what positive traits other people see, even when I don't always recognise those things in myself. Second, it gave me something to lean into and appreciate, any time I feel self-doubt creeping in. And third, it affirmed that I just need to carry on being me, doing what I'm doing, the way I'm doing it.

That short list of words is clear evidence that I *am* good enough. And so are *you*.

 Use the workbook at www.thebusinessofstories. com/magic to go through these exercises and keep a note of all the ways you can make sure the story you're telling yourself is a good one.

Yay! You've done it. What a journey we've been on together. I'm so proud of you.

 **Storytelling magic**

- The story that makes all the difference, the most important story of all is the one you're telling yourself – all day, every day.

- If you're telling yourself a story that's negative, you're unlikely to feel good about sharing it with others. You need to change that story and tell yourself a new one.

- Remember to reflect on how far you've come. Don't let the wins, the moments to cherish and celebrate, the events and people to feel grateful for slip by, unnoticed and unacknowledged.

- Your story isn't already written. You are writing it as you live it, every moment of every day.

- By creating a business that has meaning and purpose, and doing the work you love with the people you love working with, you have a legacy.

- How do you want to be remembered? How you will be remembered depends on how you show up in your life.

Conclusion

The dancer

The little girl came on stage. She had practised the short piece many times, but this was different. This was in front of all the parents and she was under a bright spotlight.

She managed the first few steps no problem, but then she stopped and froze on the spot. We all held our breath. She looked around nervously as the music continued without her. We felt her pain. Then she took a deep breath, picked up the routine again and danced the rest of the piece to the end.

When she finished, the audience cheered and whistled raucously for what felt like ages. The little girl smiled and skipped off stage.

That is what your story can feel like. Your life has not been a flawless performance. You have made mistakes. There have been times when you have felt out of your depth, frozen to the spot or unsure of what you should be doing next, but you kept going. You got through it. You came out the other side. That's the story that people will be moved by.

People appreciate real, honest stories that inspire them and leave them feeling that they too can get through the times when it all feels a bit overwhelming.

The magic of storytelling

In September 2021, a social-media campaign took the world by storm.[18] Thousands of women from around the globe told their story and shared their vulnerability to inspire young girls to march to the beat of their own drum. The campaign was initiated by Inspiring Girls International after the revelation that 70% of girls feel more confident about their future on hearing from women role models.

The stories were all different and fascinating. It soon became clear it wasn't just young girls who were inspired; many of the posts got thousands of views, likes and comments from people – young and old, male and female – who connected with the story. It

---

18 #ThisLittleGirlIsMe: https://inspiring-girls.com/thislittlegirlisme

was exciting to be a part of it, but we don't have to wait for a campaign.

Let's continue to share our stories in all their forms, so that future generations can surround themselves with and be inspired by real, authentic role models. When they read our stories, they will believe in themselves, understand their unique value and truly know that they can 'be what they can see'.

Storytelling is not an exact science. A quick search on Google would give you over 45 million results for 'How to be a better storyteller'. The only way you will ever really know if your story is going to connect the way you want it to with the people you want to work with is to share it. You need to ask the audience.

The awesome thing about storytelling is it's a skill you can start practising and honing right now. Today. Think of all the comedians who spend years showing up at open mic events and fringe theatres, trying out their material to see what makes people laugh. I'm not suggesting it's going to take you years to become a good storyteller, but you can try your stories out and see what lands. See what connects. When I'm talking to my people, I look for the nodding heads. The knowing eyes. The little smiles that say, 'Yep, that's me.' Be interested in other people's stories. Notice the ones that you connect with. Notice how they make you feel. Learn from other good storytellers.

My Circles of Storytelling Magic is the methodology I've created over the last few years, working with clients, some of whom I have featured in this book. If you've worked through it step by step, chances are you have some pretty awesome stories to share. I would encourage you to start doing that right now, if you haven't already.

If you're in doubt about where to start, a good rule of thumb is to share stories that make *you* feel something. If they make you feel something, there's a good chance they'll make your audience feel something. It's worth bearing in mind that just because a story doesn't get a ton of likes or comments, it doesn't mean people aren't engaging with it. I regularly get business owners reaching out to me because they came across my story, sometimes years before.

Whether it's told on a podcast, a blog post or at an event, people don't tend to forget a story. When the time's right, they'll get in touch. In the meantime, they could be busy telling others about you. They could be sharing your story. That's the magic of storytelling, and that's what it's ultimately about, isn't it? Stories are meant to be shared. Passed on. Passed down.

If you want raving fans out there, shouting about you and helping you reach more of the people you love to serve, you need to give them stories to share. As humans, we've been telling stories since the beginning of time, and we'll be doing it to the end of time.

Now you can be a bit more intentional about which ones you share. You've got this!

As we come to the end of this time together, I want to thank you so much for trusting me to be your guide. It's been a wild and wonderful adventure. I've loved that, for a brief moment, I've been a part of your world, and you know something? You rock. You are awesome and your stories are inspiring.

Storytelling doesn't have to be hard or complex. It's really not that scary, but man, it's so powerful. I know you're ready. If you aren't sharing your stories yet, start today. There are people out there waiting to hear them, and I want to hear them too. Please use the hashtag #thebusinessofstories so I can find them. I'll be looking out for yours.

Acknowledgements

Surrounding yourself with awesome people who inspire you and push you to be the best you can be is incredibly empowering. I am so blessed to have lots of those people in my life.

I chose my advance readers carefully, and I can't thank them enough for taking the time to give me such helpful and constructive feedback. This book is better for their input. Thank you, Karen Skidmore, Hela Wozniak-Kay, Monica Sood, Marion Ellis and Dr Anna Colton.

I've worked with many amazing clients, some of whom kindly allowed me to share their stories in this book, enabling me to bring the process to life with real-world examples. Thank you, Marion Ellis,

Skye Holland, David Wicks, Vee Tanner, Darren Higgins, Dino Tartaglia, Sherry Bevan, Ben Davis, Simon Batchelar, Cath Gough, Dr Anna and Ash Taylor.

It's exciting when you find super-talented people who can help you be even better at what you do. Jill Pryor is one of those people. She helped me create the visual elements for my brand and the graphics for this book. Thank you, Jill.

Writing this book has been fun, energising, scary and exhausting. Thank you to the team at Rethink Press who have been there for me every step of the way, cheering me on, keeping me on track and my chin up. Thank you, Lucy, Joe, Kathy and Alison.

Of course my own story goes way beyond writing this book. To get to the point where I felt qualified and ready to write the business book you now have in your hands, I've had wonderful support from many mentors and coaches. Some have helped and inspired me through the amazing content they so generously put out into the world, and some I have worked with one-to-one or in a group. Thank you, Lucy Whittington, Andrew Priestley, Richard Woods, Dan Meredith, Kevin Rogers and Donald Miller.

Finally, thank you to my gorgeous girls and incredibly patient husband, who let me hide away in my office for weeks on end to get this book written. I hope you are as proud of me as I am of you. I love you.

Contributors

The following people kindly contributed their stories to this book:

Marion Ellis – https://lovesurveying.com

Skye Holland – https://skyeholland.com

David Wicks – https://digitalhunters.co.uk

Maxine English – www.facebook.com/PartyCrownDirect

Vee Tanner – https://veetanner.com

Vanburgh Physio – https://vphysio.co.uk

Dino Tartaglia – www.successengineers.co

Sherry Bevan – www.sherrybevan.co.uk

Gary Das – www.garydas.com

Pallant Digital – https://pallant.digital

Heather Barrie – https://linktr.ee/heatherbarrie

Kingsland Wealth Management – www.kingsland-ifa.co.uk

Dr Anna Colton – www.dranna.co.uk

Ash Taylor – www.thebusinessclubhouse.co.uk

The Author

*'Storytelling in business is not just
essential, it's a superpower.'*

 From a young age Susan Payton loved stories – reading them, hearing them, telling them. Some (namely her daughters) say she was still reading stories to her children long after they wanted to read their own books and, looking back, her career has always involved elements of storytelling.

Her work in media included writing press releases at breakfast television station TV-am and researching stories for the *Chris Tarrant Breakfast Show* at Capital Radio in London. A lot of early starts for someone who is not a morning person!

As an events organiser she loved the thrill of inviting people into the story that was happening around them, and her bookshelf was full of books about storytelling long before she ever thought of it as her 'thing'.

The fact that, in later years, it has become her 'thing' was of no surprise to those who know her. Dinner with girlfriends is always filled with Susan's stories and several of her friends have been telling her for years to 'write a book'.

From her rather spectacular 'aha' moment in 2016, when the lightbulb pinged and she saw clearly what it was that she was meant to be doing, her business has thrived.

In February 2019 she became a StoryBrand Certified Guide and is the longest-standing StoryBrand Guide in the UK.

She is also proud mum to two gorgeous girls and lives on a farm in West Sussex with her husband, youngest daughter and a lot of sheep, cows and dogs.

From there, she works with business owners based all over the world, in all sorts of industries, to craft stories and narratives that launch businesses, build brands and deeply connect with their target market.

In a world where it is getting harder and harder to stand out from the crowd, Susan is passionate about showing business owners how to clearly articulate their value and speak to the right people, at the right time, with a simple message and a great story.

🌐 www.thebusinessofstories.com

in www.linkedin.com/in/susanpaytonuk

Printed in Great Britain
by Amazon

17077990R00122